To Joy

Keep playing

Praise for *Life Beyond Money*

"*Life Beyond Money* is the story of a journey, both personal and universal. In the process of telling it, Julian Freeman snaps us out of a persistent illusion, and points us towards the true source of wealth. Heartfelt and moving while remaining practical and easy to read. Enjoy!"

Jamie Smart, author of
CLARITY: Clear Mind, Better Performance, Bigger Results

"In *Life Beyond Money*, Julian Freeman takes the reader on a journey to the inside, occasionally stopping off at vantage points en route to take in the scenery and gauge his own where abouts. Reminiscent of Bill Bryson in his prime, Mr Freeman gives a moving account of his own discovery that everything is as it should be, but for our thinking that it is not."

Damian Mark Smyth, author of
Do Nothing! Stop Looking, Start Living

Life Beyond Money

Living to Earn?
Or Yearning to live?

Julian Freeman

This book is dedicated to the late and great

Hazel Levine-Freeman

A lady who truly loved us all her life

ACKNOWLEDGEMENTS

There are five seminal players in the story I am about to present to you. I had three fantastic guides and supporters who helped me gain priceless treasures and unlock my own personal treasure chest.

First, Mr. Jamie Smart (www.jamiesmart.com) the man who introduced me to the Three Principles of Mind, Consciousness and Thought. He also arranged a wonderful group of teachers in Cathy Casey, Dr Keith Blevens, Sandy Krot and Rita Shuford. Although I met him much later in my journey, I thank Dr Dicken Bettinger, too, for showing me the gifts of hopefulness and warmth.

Second, and in the same breath, I owe great thanks to Richard Wilkins and Liz Ivory (www.theministryofinspiration.co.uk) whose course *Broadband Consciousness* allowed me to see things so much more clearly. Indeed I have to thank Liz for naming the book, and Richard, you've been a powerhouse of inspiration ever since I met you. What a great gift!

The greatest of my teachers and shining above all of them is Bec Lealman - (www.beclealman.com). You showed me how to love again; a wonderful coach, mother and lover of life. You shared the largest part of this story with me. I always felt your hand strong in mine. You wanted me to "shout you from the rooftops" and I do so gladly here. B, you create magic!

And finally Lucinda Freeman. Not a player in this story in the same way as the others I've just mentioned, but my life would be fatally flawed if you weren't a part of it. You've been with me since I was a kid, a powerful connection. You've stayed constant for me throughout my life, at significant personal cost. I didn't realise quite how much of a price you paid to keep that connection alive, and that is as huge a gift as my mum's unconditional love. I love you just for that – always have, always will.

Of course, there are other great people who helped me along the way – too many to name. The list starts with my brother, Ellis Freeman: we only have a small family these days and I cherish you. Ah Dad, the next adventure is with you. I look forward to that. Thanks go to Jennifer Manson for encouraging me and helping me to publication. I really appreciate you Jen. Finally, to everyone I shared this journey with, in business, learning or living: you were all invaluable to me. It's been so great to be with you all.

My thanks and love go to each and every one of you.

Oh, and there's one special chocolate Lab who was very patient and a great companion to me for some important years.

Disclaimer: This book is written from the author's perspective and represents his story based around the events and activities portrayed; as such, it is just a story, not intended to be a statement about other people, their motives, intentions or actions.

"The past is just a thought story.
Let's set this story aside and see what is here now."
Dr Dicken Bettinger Ed.D,
Principal of 3Principlesmentoring

"It's not the absence of Thought, it's the presence of Mind."
Michael Neil, author of *The Inside-Out Revolution*

"We must be willing to let go of the life we planned
so as to have the life that is waiting for us."
Dr Joseph Campbell

PREFACE

So what is this book about anyway?

Time to Jump?

There is a old anecdote about Boiling Frogs. It's one our kids sometimes tell, an incredible story about frogs not jumping out of heating water, even as it reaches boiling point. Of course, frogs can't live in boiling water so why would they stay there? Why don't they feel the pain and just jump out? The story goes that when the water heats very slowly they just don't notice until it's too late!

Could life be a bit like that? Take a look at all the stress a lot of us live with. An ever increasing population are medicated for depression or related issues like irritable bowel syndrome and panic attacks. Why is cancer an ever increasing threat to life nowadays? Could it be a physical response to the complex and highly fast-paced lifestyle that more and more of us lead?

Why do horrific acts of violence take place in the so-called developed world, flying in the face of what I, for one, believe human nature to be? If you don't believe me, listen to the song called *Life in the Fast Lane* by the Eagles ... they nailed it over 30 years ago, and living has got a lot more intense since then.

Could it be that your life is like a backgammon game? One where the dice keep changing to double the bet and the pressure is ever increasing? Wouldn't that make you a boiling frog?

Time to change something!

Maybe you haven't quite realised what's going on. Your car needs repairing or you are a few pounds heavier (or lighter) than you used to be. Okay, you can cope with the electricity bill, the tax demand, the credit card bills and even being the "taxi service" for the kids. It's the BIG changes, like waves on the ocean of life that you really notice. A kind of, "Wow, that's a big one!" noticing.

Maybe you wonder how you are going to make it through as the waves travel toward you; a lump rises in your throat and butterflies tickle your stomach.

If you are seeing a BIG wave in your life – maybe your job is ending, you are challenged to create your own business, or your career is changing direction; maybe a relationship that was central to your life is ending, your kids are moving on or you are stepping into the responsibility of being a parent for first time.

If, like me, you see this as stepping out into the darkness, alone without a light or a map, this book is for you.

As a latecomer to the world of self-development I embarked on my own journey of self-discovery in autumn 2010. I felt rather alone, despite having a great coach in my good friend, Jamie Smart.

As I travelled my road, it occurred to me that I would have loved to know something about what to expect as the traveller, and maybe have a companion along the way. I kept that thought with me, and this book is the result.

All my experience shows me that I can't teach you anything, because you already know it; and maybe this companion will help you remember what you already know, on your journey through life. It's here to keep you company; a friend.

It could also be that there is a nugget for you within these pages, an insight, a realisation about your life that will help you along in your journey to finding real world success, contentment and satisfaction. If I've done that then I've achieved everything I set out to – and more!

How to Read this Book

I wrote this book in three parts:

Part 1 Introduction - To give you a sense of me, an everyday sub-urban man, husband, father, business man and biker, and the hero's journey that we all travel. The stage is then set for you to understand the path I was on: my road trip, if you will. Of course, my journey is not yours. Part of the fabulous thing about us humans is that we are all unique; so naturally it follows that our journeys are unique, too. But I'm sure you'll see some similarities.

Part 2 The Journey to Understanding - A selection of pieces written in the moment as I walked the path that took me to the life I live now. There are lows and high, thoughts that I held to be true and things I learned along the way. When you read them, in sections or as a whole, you will be glimpsing not just me, but the full range of the human experience that we all live through, the Ocean of Life. You'll know that you are not alone on your journey. We are all travellers. Life is one great big road trip and all you have to do is keep taking the next step.

Part 3 The Pay-off - Here I pick out some key realisations that I had about how I live my best life. If you are living the modern way, time starved and busy, busy, busy, by all means take the shortcut and read this part first. My hope is that when you get a sense of the learnings I had in my journey, you will go back and read the book in full, or at least dip into it a bit more in your free moments. That's why it's written in short chapters – to make it easy to access. In those times when you are feeling alone, why not dip into my story and remember that, actually, you aren't alone? The road has been travelled many times before.

Of course, what you will discover from this book is that your real wealth is with you at all times. Even more to the point, wealth has nothing to do with money. You never need to change, you always have everything you need to succeed, but often you don't see that in yourself – and that's all it is, seeing your life differently.

"Easy!" I hear you cry, but it's amazing how we forget that our treasures, our superpowers are with us all the time. Use this book to remind yourself that you ARE Superman, even when you feel like Clark Kent (girls, you know what I mean...)

Stillness speaks when you take time to listen

As I grew up and followed my school education I was taught to listen carefully, take notes, understand, practice and demonstrate everything. It was a system I honed at college and it powered me through to a great qualification as well as awards. I even brought a couple of friends through with me to get their degrees, too, which is something I was very proud of. I had what I thought was a really good system for approaching the world.

I'm guessing that a lot of us think like this. Certainly anyone who went through a western education would identify with it, I'm sure; but what I've found out recently is that this method misses something really essential – a feeling, a deeper understanding.

Did you just balk at what you just read? A feeling? What's that got to do with learning and education?

Two things: First, as you listen and learn in this way, you compare what you are taking in against everything you know. You test it, to see how it meets your current thinking. You can either accept it in and add it to your mental journal of everything important, or you contest it, reject it even. When you are thinking like this, are you really taking in anything new? Anthony De Mello would tell you that you are just confirming your current view; you aren't really open to new ideas and opportunities.

Anytime you respond to new input with challenge and questions, you might be blocking potential new learning. In fact, you may even feel some stress or uncomfortable feelings in response to what you are reading right now. That's a good thing. It may just mean that there is something in there for you.

Somewhere in this book you will find something that on the surface of your thinking you really don't agree with. When you get that, you've struck gold. You might have to rub off some dirt to get it, but it's there for you. Don't miss it.

The second thing is about listening for a feeling. Think about how you listen to your favourite music. When you listen to your tunes – whatever fires you up or calms you down, whatever grabs you in the moment – is it about the words and the notes or is it the feeling that you get whilst listening that really makes it enjoyable? For me, it's always been the feeling.

Listening to a person or an idea can be just the same. As you listen the way we were taught to listen at school, trying to "understand" how what you are hearing fits with what you already know, you block the possibility of hearing, and feeling, something deeper. Try "listening" to the words in this book the same way you listen to music; listen for the feeling.

Another great example of tuning in with a feeling is to just sit with someone you love – your child or your lover. When you are in a good place and you talk to them, how do you feel? Yes! Great isn't it? It almost doesn't matter what they've said, the feeling is a deeper connection.

Could you have that more in your connections to people? To life? My wish for you is that you have that feeling, from the people in your life, and from this book, too.

PART ONE

INTRODUCTION

"All the world's a stage,
And all the men and women merely players:
They have their exit's and their entrances;
And one man in his time plays many parts"

Shakespeare, *As You Like It*, Act I Scene VII

A Hero's Journey

Writing in the 16th Century, hundreds of years ago, with these words the great bard captured a quintessential insight into our life experience. We all think we are the leading actors in our own plays.

Yes, you and me. Yet we are all playing out our part in a vast stage production, one that's so BIG it makes us an infinitesimally small cameo, even when we see ourselves as centre stage with what seems like the whole world watching us from the audience. It means that life is BIG, really BIG and full of opportunity.

Even when we think our world is small and insular and the play is just us and our immediate circumstances, it's not − it's full of things that might happen on the very next page of the script. If you like, you can think of it as a play where the script isn't written until you turn the page.

This book is about one of the parts in my play, or as another great man, Dr Joseph Campbell, more recently put it, my Hero's Journey.

Now, Dr C, as I'll call him from now on, spent all his life studying and teaching the world about mythology. He distilled mythology from across many cultures and societies, across the ages, down to four basic stories. He realised that the same stories get told across all of time and are as relevant to us today as they were thousands of years ago. One of them was the "rite of passage", a major life change, the change from adolescence to adulthood. He called this kind of story the Hero's Journey, and it is relevant to all of us, any time we are going through a major change in our lives.

Let me give you a classic example to explain what Dr C meant: *Jason and the Argonauts*. It's a myth from ancient Greece – you've probably seen the Columbia Pictures movie on a Sunday afternoon. Don't you love those old movies? If you haven't seen it then it's on YouTube – go take a look.

Jason, the hero of the story, is prophesied to become the King of Thessaly. Threatened and wishing to challenge the lad, King Pelleus sets him on a quest to find the golden fleece. Guided by the goddess Hera, our hero recruits a group of other men with specialist skills and sets off to fulfil his quest. He goes through many adventures, tests and challenges to win the fleece and comes back to claim his prize in Thessaly.

Of course, that's not the end of the tale, and the way Jason gained the throne – the final twist in the story – is maybe the biggest challenge of them all.

Okay, I know you are asking: "What has this got to do with me and my hero's journey?" and "Am I really on a hero's journey?" "Am I a hero, even?"

Let's look at the plot as Dr C would see it. Something happens to our hero: a quest, a journey, comes to his or her attention. It's not necessarily of his own volition. There is a guide to send our hero on his journey – in the case of Jason, the guide is a goddess. There are a number of tests and trials before the final test. Through all of this our hero gets to see himself in a new way.

Have you ever been presented with a journey? Sure you have: starting school, becoming a parent, losing a close family member or friend, maybe? And who was there to guide you? Maybe it was a parent. Maybe it was someone who just appeared in your life at the right time to offer you the open door. Are you starting to see it yet? That you've been on a journey before?

Once you were on your journey, your hero's journey, didn't you encounter tests and trials? Did you get stressed about taking exams, did you have sleepless nights when you worried about the health of your baby, or have you had that final conversation in life with someone you held very dear?

These were all your tests. They all led to that final test, where you found out something fundamental about you... and from that moment on you lived your life very differently.

I'm sure you've got it now. You have been on these journeys before. You did it. You succeeded, just like Jason. So you ARE a hero.

Dr C tells us that we go on these journeys several times in our life. This book is about one of my hero's journeys, one of the parts I played in my theatre, as Shakespeare puts it. As you read my story, I hope you will see that you don't have to be the mighty Jason to have a fantastic adventure and to realise how you can live life in a new and more natural way for you.

It's all about living your best life. That's my wish for you as you step out to read the rest of this book. But first, I need to tell you a bit more about me, the hero in this particular journey.

My Jewellery - My Story

If you had asked me many years ago whether I would be a big wearer of jewellery, I definitely would have said, "No"; but as I wake up today and get dressed I realise that every day includes quite a bit of silverware.

It's like I collect my awards again and show them off to the world. Actually, that's a great feeling. My jewellery represents the milestones in my life − my personal story − a story that's worth telling here and now.

My first and most treasured piece is a leather and silver band that my mum gave me. It came from a necklace of three identical pieces: one she kept, one went to my brother and the last piece to me. The tradition carries on, too, as my son wears one of the pieces today.

As I lay it out before me now, strong and straight, I see how Mum was the backbone to my life − always there for me, in support. This piece means so much to me and I love wearing it.

My earliest memory of her is walking hand in hand in the snow tracks to kindergarten, so that my winter boots didn't fill up. The snow was so deep for a little guy like me. The sky was warm and full of grey, snow-filled clouds. It was a magical journey; just Mum and me.

My dad? Well he was always marching off to the train for London to work hard and become the successful international businessman he always deserved to be. The most I saw of him was deadheading rose bushes before he left for the station on a summer's morning.

Later, when I was about thirteen, my dad started working abroad for long periods and after a number of years my parents split up. My dad left my life for a while after that, but Mum was always there.

Mum had four great sayings that sum up the support she gave her boys. How about these words in troubled times?

"It's all going very well."
"Everything happens for a reason."
"Something good will come out of this."

And then when life changed for the positive:

"That's brilliant!"

Try using a few of these from time to time. I'm sure you get a sense of just how fantastic a supporter she was ... until the time came for me to support her.

In August 2009 she was diagnosed with cancer and I joined her team, along with my brother, Ellis, and her lifelong friend, Joan Wall, for the next seven months as she fought the good fight and made her exit in her own unique way. It sounds strange to say it, but this was a quality time. Our relationship was at its best, its closest, a time when I could give back all the love and support she had given me over the years. Even though she was very ill and I was fitting in a demanding working week, I look back on those months as the most special times.

Interestingly, when I first told this story to a group I said, "When my life died … no, when my mum died". I think that says it all. Thank you, Mum.

The next piece of jewellery is a blue stone ring in silver, a present from my wife in our early twenties. It saw me through thirty years of young love, business and adventure. It reflects our hopes and dreams together, how she stood by me through everything, good and bad. That was huge for me.

While I was a student, she played successful TV star. Then she married me and within a few years we became Mum and Dad. She was particularly good at it, filling in all the gaps while I pursued my career. Climbing that ladder was important to me – scaling those heights. For all the roles she played, for her steadfastness, her understanding, and just for being my best friend for thirty-some years, I owe her a massive vote of thanks. It's only fitting to record that for everyone to see, here in these pages.

At school I just didn't fit the system. I remember the headmaster having me into his office at the end of the year to tell me I must try harder, just when all his other appointments were to congratulate the great and the good.

Everything changed for the better when I started as an apprentice engineer. I tutored some of my peers through college and that helped me do well. "In teaching you will learn," they say. I ended up in the top three of my year in all the engineering courses and with awards for the best graduate apprentice. Not a bad turnaround, huh?

My career rocketed forward, sideways and forward once more. A large part of my life became about business, or more specifically, success in business.

The very short story is that I went from apprentice to university star, to working with computers at the start of that boom, then progressed to customer service director in the middle of the dotcom bubble. I've built businesses and sold them; I've retired three times and still the rollercoaster continues.

Somewhere along the line I paid off my mortgage, bought lots of motorbikes for me and horses for the rest of the family. This was my personal backgammon game. Can you see the bet doubling again and again? I certainly did!

Success, yes. Even I read this story and say to myself, "That's pretty successful, by any standards". But I'd missed lots of my family life, kids events at school and so on. I'd travelled a lot and been away from home, all in the name of ambition and bringing home the bacon. Satisfaction – yes and no. Does this sound familiar? I guess a lot of us live with a precarious balance to our lives. One that we aren't quite comfortable with.

I seemed to spend all my time in remembering the past or worrying about the future and was hardly ever here. How can you live your life without ever being present? I did ... do you?

They were heady days in business, and I had the clothes to match. I even had the cuff links to match the ring, especially designed to go with the impressive Hugo Boss suits I wore in the 90s. What days!

Next up in my jewellery inventory is my Celtic band thumb ring. Thinking about this takes me straight back to Westminster School where my son, age 11, was doing his entrance exam. Even though he and I both knew we were only really doing it for his grandfather, we were pleased to be there. He went into the exam room; it was a sunny summer's morning and I had three hours to kill. On an impulse, I went to Soho and bought the ring from a company called Crazy Pig Designs.

I didn't wear this ring for a long while. I worried about what it might say about me. Now I wear it proudly because it represents me, my son and my family. My daughter, Helen, also has a couple of great pieces from Crazy Pig — I love sharing that with her. Shouldn't everyone squeeze the juice out of little things like that? Sure they should.

I found my wife young, we set up home together and then became Mummy and Daddy, as people do. For years we travelled a fantastic road from lovers to life companions. We found the stars and followed our dreams together with a passion that endured during all those changes.

Helen, my daughter, has always been more linked with her mum — maybe we inherited that from my wife's matriarchal Scottish family. Of course, I went to watch my daughter ride every weekend, and I took my son to football, rugby and later riding, too. I loved watching him play. "Better than watching the National Team!" I would declare to anyone who would listen.

He was always mildly embarrassed as I shouted loudly from the touch lines, but those were golden times — especially poignant when I remember that all my childhood activities had been done on my own. I wanted more for my kids and I'm so glad they got it.

All through those years I wore a Celtic wing necklace. That stands for bikes, freedom, feeling young and my own personal space; all the reasons why I had five motorcycles in the end. However hard things got, with business or family, bikes were my escape.

They are still an important part of my life, but I don't need a garage-full to complete me nowadays – all I need is two wheels and an engine. As soon as I fire it up I'm eighteen again. Wonderful!

A piece of jewellery that almost everyone wears – if they're over thirty – is a watch. Mine was a gift on my 40th birthday. We were on a sailboat in the Caribbean to celebrate my second coming of age: my family, father, brother with his partner, and me, soaking up the sunshine and the sea. They bought me the most expensive versions of all my favourite things: my brother, a silver bracelet, my wife, top of the range Oakley sunglasses and a Tag Heuer watch.

I tried to love their gifts even though the sunglasses hurt to wear and the watch wasn't what I would have chosen. I wanted to receive them in the spirit they were given, but I couldn't. Does that sound spoilt and ungrateful? It does to me, too, but I got a sign shortly after that, to make my own choices, when the watch mysteriously disappeared; I got to replace it with another great watch, the one I chose. In hindsight it seems that choosing was starting to rear its head as something I needed to do more of, the universe nudging me into learning those lessons.

I have a beautiful photo somewhere of us sailing along, boat heeled over, everyone smiling and a fantastic seascape behind. A picture so good it should be in the holiday brochure. The dream situation, you're thinking? I totally agree with you.

I'd travelled a long and quite successful road – but it wasn't all sweetness and light. I'd been playing the western materialist game, and the hunter-gatherer, too. It reminds me of Tevya in that great old movie *Fiddler on the Roof* where he goes on his rounds every day, without fail. If his poor horse is lame he looks after it and pushes the cart himself. It's a good life, if that's what you've chosen. But I suddenly realised that I hadn't chosen; instead I'd become a Boiling Frog.

It became clear to me that I'd been carried away by a different tide. My parents had very different beliefs about what money means and how it should be used. Did you know that you can have loads of money and still be deeply worried about things like security and control over your life circumstances? These were very strong currents for my parents, born from their parents' fortunes and life experiences.

My money story was handed down to me with a twist of Maggie Thatcher's consumerist society and a dash of the American dream added to taste. That was a heady cocktail! I was so busy making it all happen, balancing the books and keeping it all together, that life was just passing me by. Every year it felt like forty-six weeks just went past and six weeks were actually memorable. Hold on, shouldn't all fifty-two weeks be memorable?

I realised that I was far more myself on the deck of a sailboat than thinking about birthday gifts. I was far more relaxed walking my dog on the beach, even if the skies were leaden grey, than when I sat in big business meetings or played the corporate game. What I learned when I got money is that real wealth is having the time to be me – really me.

I thought about how I could live my life following that new flow. It's a subtler current, but one that's much more natural and requires much less effort: I call it "semi-retirement".

I love what I do and don't want to give that up. Hell, I'm good at it! So I set out to change the way I do what I do to make more of a positive impact on the world AND have loads more time for me.

That's how my Heart Forever ring arrived. It came from Crazy Pig (again) and I wear it on my wedding ring finger. It's like a new marriage, a perfect partnership – me with life. It's all about me treating life like an adventure once again, this time as the true me and not someone bullied by expectation and pressure from society and my peers.

This ring marks the time when the book *Synchronicity* came to me. It's a fantastic book by Joe Jaworski, about life unfolding with perfect timing. I marvelled in the story, one of fantastic success in great causes – it sounded just right to me. The only part that didn't ring true for me was where he meets his new partner for life – Mavis – and then my Mavis arrived!

Synchronicity fitted so closely with my new life, the life beyond, beyond my thoughts and feelings about money. My story didn't play out exactly the same way as Mr Jaworski's, a different synchronicity was to be mine, but life was playing its dance with me, all the same.

My jewellery tells my story. I see all of these parts of the story as strong positives in my life. They all combined to get me here. It's all good, especially my last addition: Heart Forever.

Maybe that will be the title for book two of my story. I wonder what jewellery I'll be wearing then. Maybe I won't need any jewellery at all? We'll see..

Bikes and me

I have to tell you about bikes – the two wheels, no pedals, big engine variety. I love 'em!

I've ridden since I was sixteen. If I didn't have a girlfriend I always had my bike. Exciting and much more reliable, too. My bike was always waiting in the garage, looking beautiful, to thrill me with an adrenaline-filled journey.

I've done sports bikes on race tracks; I can show you pictures of me with my knee skimming the Tarmac at 80 or 90 on a corner or doing 170 down a long straight, tucked in tight while all the other riders move into slow motion. "Warp speed Mr Sulu?" Yes, I do dare.

I can show you a picture of a bike I rode on Millennium Day, too. It was fifty degrees and I rode in just a t-shirt on January 1st.

There is something about riding a bike that's so puts you out in the world, whether it's driving from the bottom of the mountain, where it's hot, to the top, feeling the change in temperature to cool or snow even. Maybe it's being up in a high pass and turning the corner to have hundreds of vultures wheeling in the sky just above your head. My favourite is riding the mountains in Andalusia, leaving the rainy central plains, climbing on beautiful wide roads and basking in the heat of southern Spain. Breathe deep and take in the wonderful and powerful smell of the olive groves.

The bikes themselves, too. The BSA, full of old British character while vibrating your hands off the handlebars. A Buell like Steve McQueen rode, ready to jump the wires in *The Great Escape*. My Yamaha R1 Sports bike, egging me on to more speed every ride. My Harley Electra Glide, a royal limo; and the looks from other drivers when I was on my Harley v-rod. Each one different, beautiful and something I loved to own.

There's just something about bikes and me. At one point I would have told you that if I had a vice it was bikes. Lucy, my wife, would certainly agree. I found Lucy because of a bike.

I remember her looking out from her full face helmet with those piercing blue eyes, casually wearing a tied-up cheese-cloth shirt, looking so sexy, or shaking her long hair free from her helmet to the jaw-dropping stares of my friends. Wow, what a great way to find a fantastic girl!

I love the paraphernalia as well. My track pictures have me in leather from head to toe, brightly coloured, like a medieval knight at the joust. The clothes are technical, too – it's a bit sci-fi, like wearing gadgets. I can never have enough gloves or helmets – a guy's got to have a choice, you know. Is it about the conditions? Hmm ... no, it's all about how it makes me feel. It's a bit like a girl's fetish for shoes.

I have one great memory of when bikes and girls meet. A fleeting instant with me in full racing leathers hugging a beautiful Austrian lady, just risen from her bed, all purple gauze and fresh soap. Leather meets silk, muscle meets poise. A moment and then a memory, a fantasy, never to be repeated.

I don't have any bad memories of bikes. None. Even after a couple of crashes and a ropey left knee, I just couldn't imagine life without one. They put you in the moment, really feeling the road, not the destination, just as far as you can see in this instant. They connect you with yourself. Your senses tingle, you are completely open to the world. The thrill of it is massive – cruising or racing, it doesn't matter. And that's the real joy of bikes: not the ownership, not the paraphernalia, not the memories. You just jump on, start up, turn onto the road and ... freedom!

It all seemed so Real

Okay, so one more thing before I start telling this tale. It's something that I must mention first, as it is a central realisation for us all.

I have a favourite saying that history is not about the facts or the truth, it's really about how it was recorded and interpreted after the fact by the historians and their patrons.

Some things cannot be denied: that millions of Jews, gypsies, Slavs and other ethnic groups were slaughtered in the 1940s; that commercial airplanes did crash into and destroy the World Trade Centre in New York City on 9/11. We can't argue those facts.

Some things are less certain. Did man land on the moon? I like to believe so, but for a long time there was a quite widely held conspiracy theory that it was all faked. "But there was TV footage," I hear you say? So? I could edit footage, add a commentary with credible people taking part and I bet you'd believe it! Watch a 1980s movie called *Capricorn 1* and you'll see what I mean. It might sound far-fetched, but could Princess Diana be lying on a beach somewhere sipping a cocktail in peace? I'd like to think so. Who really knows these days?

So what about your history?

You are your own historian. Your thoughts are how you interpret the facts in the moment. That shapes your reality as you live it. The decisions you make are all about how you see it, and not necessarily what was there.

Hold on! This is BIG. To show you what I mean, let me ask you to cast your mind back to some event in your life where you did something, accidentally upset a friend or messed up with a partner. You didn't want it to go the way it happened, but it did. In hindsight you can see how you would have decided differently if you had known then what you know now – but at the time it seemed to you like you were doing the right thing.

Start to see that what you think about things creates how you see them – your experience of life. This applies to memories, too. Those aren't the facts either; they are how you store and access certain situations. Remember that old saying: "seeing through rose-tinted spectacles". A great example of this might be the birth of a child, where the pain of childbirth, so real as it happens, is completely replaced at the time and over time by the joy of meeting the new child. The pain is completely forgotten, but the joy is always remembered.

Memories shape our story about ourselves. They are how we see ourselves, what we think we are good at or not good at. They can hold pain and joy in whatever measure we want to add it. Somehow they can also shape our actions today and in the future. I don't think of myself as a good dancer, for example. So I don't dance. Maybe I am unnecessarily denying myself one of life's simple pleasures? Have you ever stopped to ask yourself whether the story you tell yourself is the best story for you? What if you could change that story? In an instant? But that's a whole book in itself ...

It's our thoughts and memories, let me call those habitual thoughts, that make us all truly unique. We all think differently, day-to-day, moment-to-moment. And it's new thought that opens us up to the possibilities that life has for us "waiting in the wings". The rest of what you will read here is the way I saw it at the time, coloured in by my memory, hindsight and softened with the passing of time. It's uniquely my version of my life experience. I'm sure that others who know parts of this tale would tell it differently. I'm okay with that and I hope they will be, too. Nobody is lying; everyone is telling their truth.

Having said all that, we are ready to begin. So let's go.

PART TWO

THE JOURNEY

TO UNDERSTANDING

"I must go down to the seas again, to the lonely sea and the sky,
And all I ask is a tall ship and a star to steer her by,
And the wheel's kick and the wind's song and the white sail's shaking,
And a grey mist on the sea's face, and a grey dawn breaking."

John Masefield
(English Poet Laureate, 1930-1967)

Carving

This is my dream of snowboarding like a pro. The reality is −
and I'm the first to admit it − I snowboard badly; but it's still
great! Have you ever been skiing or boarding? Maybe you can
relate ...

The sun shines across the big view
My goggles gleam green in return
Down the steep slope we go
Shoulder turning
Board sweeping
Edge biting
Choosing our lines to match the mountain
Giving us our speed
A wholesome flow
To dance us to the valley floor below

Pitch and turn
Pitch and turn
Pitch and turn
We glide across and with the hill
Flatter here and steeper there
Earth meets sky meets board and I
A magic trail to weave its spell
And leave me smiling once again

I started snowboarding somewhat late in life, at forty, full of
fear. I was a tentative boarder, I dug for my edges, I braked hard
before every turn. I fell over a lot! I wondered why was it so
painful and so tiring. Surely boarding should be fun? Maybe I'll
stick to bikes.

My son, Ben, started boarding at the same time as me. He was
seven, no fear, and after a few trips to the mountains he was
streaking down the slopes, whooping! He could do three or four

runs for my one, and while I was tired he was eager for more.

When the power goes through the edge and into the snow, you are balanced and safe; when you brake hard and don't let the board go you are wobbly, and a fall – the last thing you want – is just a moment away.

I'm learning to carve. Slowly I use less edge, until I come to a really difficult part of the mountain – and then the brakes are back on. Still, it's getting better and I'm enjoying it more. I love the altitude and the views, too. There's something just amazing about looking down on the world from on high ...

Maybe the board symbolised life for me? I had a strong tendency NOT to let the board run. I paid for it – it was really hard work! It means I miss the view, too, and the fantastic experience, whilst battling all the way down.

It felt like my life had been like that for many years and I was very tired of it. How could what was meant to be such an exhilarating ride be so painful and frustrating? Maybe, I thought, it's time to do it differently? Time to let the board run a bit more, to feel that balance and power.

The Dominica Question

My dad always wanted me to go on Safari with him. He loves, loves, loves Africa.

It's a two-week trip and for most of that time you have no email or mobile phone. In all the years I was in business I hadn't taken more than a week off at a time. Being uncontactable felt wrong – I couldn't possibly leave the business for that long! So I didn't go.

Then after my mum died and I sold my business interests, I didn't have that excuse any more; so the next time Dad asked, I agreed to go. That was September 2010.

We flew to Joburg, collected a van and drove north to Botswana, stopping for supplies in Polokwane. It's the last major town in the Limpopo province and growing fast, a heady mix of seven day retailing and ladies in their traditional church uniforms going to service. We fuelled the van and I drank weird cappuccino: Roibos tea with frothy milk and chocolate on top. Yuck!

Another day's journey had us fording the Limpopo river and driving the red dust roads, taking us to the home of the free and uncomplicated animals. It's a different world out there, where the cycle of seasons and nature rule, man just a bystander, an interloper.

We watched the animals, but they just had a passing interest in us. I didn't miss the outside world; in fact I laughed when someone suggested a drive over to a hill a few miles away to get phone signal.

During hours of travelling, my thought ranged far and wide, through our family relationships and my new possibilities. One idea I had was that if I sold everything we could move to the Caribbean and retire. We had money for many years and I was sure that we could make it work. I saw us in shorts and sandals, sipping a drink in the early evening sunset, a dream we could easily make real.

On a visit to the beautiful island of Dominica we had done a full tour in a tiny minibus. The driver was a character, like they all seem to be out there – he had five kids, he told us, all by different women. He showed us the rainforest, we enjoyed the volcanic springs, ate great local food on the side of a mountain and listened to reggae. There was always music, happy music, uniquely Caribbean.

He took us high up on a bluff on the Atlantic side of the island where the palms swayed in the trade winds and the rollers crashed to the shore far below. The view was unbelievable and the plot was for sale, affordable. It was all possible, now.

As we drove through South Africa, the dream started to take shape. We could grow pineapple, avocado, bananas right in our back yard, a slice of heaven on Earth. Just the thought of it made me smile. The more I thought about it, the easier it seemed.

That night at dinner I light-heartedly raised the question; Lucy responded very strongly, saying there were a thousand reasons why we couldn't go. Still light-hearted, I asked her to name them. She blustered a bit but it was abundantly clear I'd struck a nerve. Up until that moment I hadn't realised the distance that had grown between us in recent times. How had this happened to us? We'd always been so close and aligned in our journey together. Or had we? This was a significant moment, more than a storm in a teacup, but in true British style, with stiff upper lip, we avoided the obvious. I backed off – after all, how serious was I? We got on with the holiday and at the time I thought no more about it. We had a great time, as we usually do when we get together as a family.

Looking back on this now, this dream, this question, this conversation, was the start of something. I'm not sure I realised it at the time. There's a moment in the film *Jurassic Park*, when the first thud of the footstep of a tyrannosaurus Rex is heard, and water in a cup on the car dashboard ripples. This was like that, a portent. Something was coming that was going to change things for all of us.

After my mum's death, and free from the constant pressure of business, I was ready for change. Was I the only one? That thought niggled at me. Looking back, I see it as the call to go on my journey, although it was some months yet before I would start.

My Inner Compass

Later that year I met the great Jamie Smart. He was doing an exercise about listening for a feeling at a big conference in London. In the same way that I talked about how you listen to music, in this exercise, in conversation with a partner, you listen, not to the words that are being spoken, but to the feeling that lies beneath the words. It was a powerful experience, and I felt a deep sense of connection with the person I was working with, till that moment a complete stranger. For the few minutes of the exercise I experienced something new and I wanted more: I wanted guidance. I signed up for Jamie's group.

Over the course of the next few months I started to get a sense of what I called my "inner compass". The first thing I discovered was that it was pointed in a different direction to where I had been heading for the last twenty years. This was a shock, and at the same time I realised I must have known this all along; for reasons of family, of duty, of obligation, I'd been ignoring the compass, had put it away. Now I could see it again I was compelled to take notice.

As I started to follow my compass, my intuition, my wisdom, I got glimpses of a very different me. I became so sure of myself, and comfortable in my own skin. I remember one particular moment, when I was picking a partner to work with in one of Jamie's exercises. I felt an amazing energy filling my chest and shoulders, ready to burst out from my red A&F t-shirt and radiate round the room. My feet were planted, solid, and I felt like Hercules, able to carry the world with ease.

This was what it was like to follow my compass and truly be me; I wanted more of this feeling.

For months I'd used my old college strategies to make sense of what Jamie was teaching, but actually, this inner compass is not something you need to learn. It's already there, always operating, pointing True North. I just had to see that, for life, for me, to change.

Other people in the group noticed it, my energy, my power. I attracted people to work with. Mostly women. I'd never been attractive to women, well, not in the last twenty years anyway, no doubt partly because I'd taken myself off the market. I wasn't trying to make anything happen. I was just revelling in being me – just me – and everyone around me saw it and felt it.

One Sunday, at one of Jamie's weekend workshops, as we were choosing partners for one of the exercises, a guest at the event stomped straight up to me, stood right in front of me and declared, "I want to work with you!" I had met B. Her grey eyes sparkled, exactly matching the way I felt. It was like magic! We did the exercise together, then both had lunch with the rest of the group; it was sunny, a great day, and I knew I wanted more of this.

Going home was a huge contrast. With my newly rediscovered compass I knew that home and duty were not the right direction. But surely that couldn't be right? I fought it, but I just knew something wasn't right. There was a tension, a pull, urging me in a new direction, and I couldn't ignore it. The Dominica question had been my call to take the hero's journey; this was me crossing the threshold and starting out.

The Real You

Ever taken morphine or heroine?

I had a bike accident once. I was lying on a spinal board in Accident & Emergency and the doctor asked me to rate my pain. One to ten.

"Six, maybe seven," I told him. Good old British stiff upper lip.

"We'll make you more comfortable."

The effect of the morphine was instantaneous, like a wave through my body. I had a strong urge to struggle, to run away from it, but the spinal board meant I couldn't move at all. The strange sensation coursed through me, up towards my head and face.

... and then calm, peace, endless time. Why had I worried and panicked so?

Remembering me was just like that ...

I had held myself in control for many years, my whole adult life. Now I opened myself to life, I allowed myself to be more real: no more stiff upper lip or being the archetypal father and husband. It felt good.

I thought I could control it. I didn't realise how far it would continue, to the point where I felt naked, new born.

There were times when I just didn't recognise me as the person I had been. Like the morphine taking me over, it was scary, but the peace, the knowing and the joy that came after were awesome. A deep inner calm and contentment with me.

I think this is what people call "awakening", but to me it is more natural than that. Somewhere deep down inside you is a perfect you that is waiting to be remembered. The true you, that will live the blissful life that you were meant to live. It's just like Joseph Campbell said. We've just forgotten, got weighed down by unnecessary conditioning.

I wondered at this new person I had become. I hardly recognised myself – but that's fine, just go with it, it's the most natural thing in the world. Making that shift, you might find that you live differently, but what's wrong with that? It might be a lot better than the life you were living, for you and everyone around you. Others may not like parts of the real you, but they adjust, just like you do. It's all good.

You follow the path of bliss, of just being you. You're a better person than you've ever been before. It's effortless. Little kids are great at it, so why can't adults do that, too?

The Tower of Babble

How different was this new place? It was different and the same. You see I never really lost me. I was always there. I had just forgotten who I was.

I know a man, a very successful man, just coming up to his seventy-fifth birthday. He is a great thinker and an intellectual, successful throughout his life: he had a scholarship at school, and as a top-rank finance man he played the corporate financing "game" at the highest level for many years – you know the kind of guy, if not from life, then from the movies. Add to all that a fantastic wealth of reading and life experience and there isn't anything he hasn't got a great piece of advice for. And the best thing of all, he's my father.

My dad brings to mind for me that old Bible story of the Tower of Babel, only I call it the Tower of Babble. As I see it, he's spent seventy-five years building a structure of thinking, each piece carefully placed, a thing of beauty. Imagine being inside a wonderful cathedral, each vault and column a life experience, a learning, a decision.

I stand in awe of the structure he's built. From the bedrock foundations of his values, his longest and deepest-held beliefs about "quality people", his honesty and integrity, to the flying buttresses of his ideals for the world, his services to charity, it all looks perfect. A fantastic piece of carefully crafted architecture, imposing and ready to last a millennium.

Exactly as it should be. Until I realise that his cathedral is not mine.

My world, my thinking, is more like a forest, a wild western wood, totally natural and organic. I have some big trees, like my business career. Some of the older ones have fallen over and died in the winter storms, but that is how nature goes.

I have beautiful young trees, too: my kids as they grow and develop, the new lover in my life. I survey the beauty of my forest, from the crunch of the wet mould underfoot, the gently falling autumn leaves as the seasons turn, to the wind in the branches giving me fresh air and space to breathe.

Whereas my father is an architect, building, shaping and planning his life experience, I am a forester, working with what is there for me, nurturing and marvelling at the beauty and perfection of nature, not quite sure how the wood will be in the future, but knowing that whatever is will be wonderful.

I don't have the shelter or protection of a stone building, I'm open to the elements – or that's how it feels.

Who is right?

We both are – and that's the wonder of the human experience. We share genes, but our thinking is totally different. I see his building and don't want to live there; he worries that I don't have anything substantial and will get caught by the elements.

We respect each other – we love each other – and we try to see each other's world, knowing that it is important to each of us. We live our lives, separately mostly, together on occasion and know that we play a significant role for each other.

To me, my father is the baobab tree I touched in Botswana. So huge that it towers beyond anything else in the valley. The only one of its kind. Big enough to shelter me. Beautifully formed, but quite bare except for the rare occasions when it flowers. It is awe inspiring; he is awe inspiring.

So why did I mention the Tower of Babble? To show that we both have thinking, but it works differently for each of us. Our thoughts are our illusions. Is my father's thinking solid as stone? Is my wood really so wild? Everyone thinks in different ways, just like in the Bible story.

We have the power to transform our thoughts, the way we see life, in a moment. The way we see life can change forever. My baobab tree couldn't exist in a European wood, but my thinking allows me to imagine it. There are no rules when it comes to thinking. I could be imagining a Caribbean beach, palm trees, bubbling surf and all.

And then we have consciousness; I have my awareness of the whole wood, I'm not lost in the trees. He has the ability to see his cathedral as part of a skyline. That's the real power. Then we see the same sun and sky; our shared world.

So often we are caught up in the next extension to the building or in husbanding a tangled part of the wood, and we forget the beauty of what we have, we don't take the time to wander and admire the world. And then we stop, look up and remember. That's when we see what life is really all about.

Perhaps I'd been comparing myself to my dad, and that made me feel I should be someone else, or doing something else. He had been so successful, how was I ever going to get anywhere near him? I knew I wouldn't be able to, and it weighed on me; and I had compared myself to others, too,

Starting the search for me felt good, it felt important. I had forgotten me for so long.

Dessert island discs

As my internal journey really got under way I started thinking more and more about leaving. I did that a lot in the early days, imagining packing a bag, just a few essentials, and going; anywhere warm – freedom

I'd have no loved ones to entangle me in their wants and needs, no pretences to keep up for someone else's sake. Of course, I knew that was all inside me – I conjured up conversations that hadn't even happened with these other people – I could even hear their voices saying the words; but it wasn't them holding me in, it was me.

They said they had imagined conversations with me, too. The clouds of stories were thick around me, like a fog, until it was hard to see anything clearly any more. It was hard to know me. I had played every game but my own, and I still wasn't where I wanted to be.

Time to leave. Time to ride. I'd pack the big Harley and follow the rallies for the rest of the summer. Solitude was always my friend when I was young; it never made any demands of me, a quiet companion. No need to impress, nobody to worry about, just me and the open road, the mountains and the sky. Ride until it's time to stop, in a place that feels right.

I'd start fresh and new – a clean slate! Of course, I knew my music would go with me, full of emotion and memories. That's one thing that always works for my good, buoys me up and sends me forward; a gift from thousands of talented people, and I'm so grateful.

Maybe I'd sail, captain a bareboat in the Caribbean, where every day is perfect, warm sun on tanned skin; the thrill of wind in sails, a modest beer at the end of the day.

I'd go to a place where nobody told me what to do. I didn't need to learn anything and there was no path to follow. 'Maybe there aren't a thousand paths to choose from after all?' I thought. 'Maybe that's an illusion and the best path is none at all?' I imagined a perfect and simple life.

I just wanted an escape. My food looked wrong, and I couldn't walk the dog without creating situations in my head that didn't exist. Something had to change. Escape seemed like a realistic and viable option.

Along the way, I might meet my other old friend, loneliness. He's always knocking to come in when I'm on my own for a while. I'm used to him and his mate, longing. These are great friends, although sometimes they don't feel like it. They shake me out of my reverie and remind me that one person, alone and withdrawn from life and love, is not enough.

With all this backwards-and-forwards thinking, I stayed where I was, leaving this proposal on the table time and time again, unopened. I'd think about it for a few hours, then I'd go out and live my life – my new life, as the new me. People didn't recognise me. Some saw me as selfish, others worried about what was happening to me or wanted me back "in my box".

It was time to be bigger than I had been. I wasn't trying to pick a fight with anyone; I didn't need anyone's approval. I never intended to hurt anyone, but I needed to be all that was in me, bursting to come out, like sunshine.

I felt guilty about the effect this had on the people I'd cared for for so long. They understood least of all. The pressure in the middle of this was huge, and once again I was tempted to leave. "Why don't I? What am I scared of?"

I asked this question every time I was in this place. I wasn't scared of who I was or where my life was leading me – it was only about the change. Like learning to wheelie a motorcycle: it seems scary and then you're doing it. A simple three-step process and you're there.

Trying to layer new thinking on my old life was like adding to a huge house of cards: it had become way too complex for even me to figure out. I just wanted to take out a pickaxe and shatter these illusions. Make it simple. I've noticed that for me, that's when life works best. Just do what is right for now, this instant and that moves me forward. If I did that, each step would then be my best life.

I was at the edge of a cliff, looking out over the chasm, but I wasn't quite ready to jump.

Here, there and everywhere

You know that song by the Beatles? That really captured this moment for me.

Over the next few weeks life started to unfold for me in a new and different way. I met B several times. Each and every time, electricity arced between us and I felt life so strongly.

She sat with me on a leather sofa in Costa on the motorway one day, her presence astounding me, her words plunging a knife deep into my heart.

I visited her in the West Midlands and found her standing on tiptoes like an excited teenager, a broad grin on her face, anticipating our warm embrace.

Our conversations were so real, so true, so meaningful. I wanted life to be like this every day. The depth of her wisdom was new to me, intoxicating. I hung on her words, drinking them in: "We spend so much of our time planning, setting goals, attempting to control the outcomes, attempting to control our life ... You see, there are so many possibilities, so many beautiful opportunities if we take the blinkers of life off, if we allow something new and wonderful to come to us ..."

We met again at another coaching event, and just couldn't be parted. Even thought we sat in different places in an auditorium of hundreds of people our eyes met knowingly and words didn't need to be spoken. Placing ourselves at a distance, I always sat behind her so I could see her. I just couldn't get enough. B turned round to look often in my direction and when our eyes met there were sparks. It was magical.

B stood up to speak and there was a serenity to her in that moment that held everyone in the room. They all heard the depth of her truth and felt the power of her love. Many people were drawn to connect with her afterwards. It felt like I'd just heard the most inspirational speaker ever.

The rest of the event was a bit of a blur. We enjoyed our friends and the sunshine and each other. I recall so distinctly the moment when I got B to sit on my lap and she was thrilled by the daring of it – being seen together, officially. I didn't care.

Then it was time to part, leave the perfect weekend; take the strong connection with us. The feelings in me just got stronger and stronger. There was an innocence, a beautiful naivety, I hadn't felt like this for many years. This was my new direction, I was sure of it.

I went back and explained to my family: to Lucy, to Ben, to Helen. It was hard. Very hard. They cried. I cried. They didn't understand or want me to go. I think it was a complete sideswipe for Lucy. She'd trusted me for so long and I'd been so constant in her life that to this day I don't believe she expected anything like this. Although she wore it well in front of me I'm sure it was as hard for her as the kids, if not more so. In lots of ways I didn't want to leave them either.

Duty, responsibility, loyalty and love all urged me to stay, but I knew I had to go, to discover something in me. A new life beckoned. But before that I was going to run with the bulls!

———

Riding free

For some time I'd planned a motorcycle road trip. There's nothing like it. The way you experience the world is just magical. I'd got together a group of guys to share it with and in June 2011 I led them on a journey across Europe.

Years before I'd seen the old town of Pamplona from a distance, and I knew I needed to go back there. The Bull Run created the moment; the time was now.

It was perfect. I needed space to think more clearly, to live completely differently. Dressed in black leather, white t-shirt, booted and buckled, hair sharp, I piloted the big black Electra Glide under hot blue skies. French chateaux, long straights with tin boxes waiting for me to pass them in style. Flowing bends bordered by sunflowers and vineyards. My mind emptied – marvellous.

We rode down the west coast of France. St Malo, Rennes, Nantes, Lucon, Royan and ended up just south of Bordeaux. We stopped off at the oyster beds on the Gironde. Effortless, easy, no stress. Freedom to connect the bike with the road. It was pure joy. I whooped out loud and breathed big breaths of sunshine.

This was the true me. Clear and joyous. Authentic. No thoughts to constrain me. Something to savour, it nourished my spirit. Freedom. Priceless. A gift beyond words. Now I could speak my words and make my path. Instead of following the SatNav slavishly I followed my senses, followed the road.

Then the Pyrenees appeared from the haze. Even from a distance they looked big, the power of a mountain range. What followed was real riding. The route I chose was right through the middle of the range: three cols, all at 1600 metres plus. Let's not mess around. I wanted to know the full summer spirit of the Pyrenees.

Pretty soon I was leading the group up small steep roads, higher and higher. No barrier protected our journey. Small tunnels were wet with mountain stream water. Woods gave way to grass and then to bare rock marked with a little snow. It was sunny and hot at the top. Col de Soulor done! We were all elated, amazed by the ride we'd just done and looking forward to more.

We left the friendly sheep and horses on the Col de Soulor and followed narrow undulating roads that hugged the side of the mountain to the Col d'Aubisque; there were fantastic views back down into France, a long, long way below. And then we were at the summit.

Quick coffee, small nap in the sunshine, then the descent. Winding, flowing, almost steeper down than up. Just point the bike and steer. Left, right, left to the bottom. Some of the guys took off to challenge themselves and feel the elation of it all. I just cruised. I was centred, chilled, free to ride.

Next were the overhanging gorges, along mountain streams to the Col d'Tarblet. This was a higher, more open road. Faster and faster we rode, to the Spanish border where the eagles greeted us. It was a fantastic day's riding. On down big winding roads, the mountains retreating behind us.

Done. Completed. Conquered. Everything the mountains could throw at me. I took my helmet off and gave thanks to our guides. I laughed now, where in the weeks before I might have cried. Both are good, but now I had space and time and laughter flowed from me. This wasn't a holiday or a vacation – this was the start of a new life. I revelled in the adventure.

Running with the Bulls - Pamplona 2011

Normally on a road trip the destination is just the excuse for the ride, but my stay in Pamplona became an adventure within an adventure.

During the festival everyone dresses in white and red, for the protection of Saint Fermin. It's the biggest gathering in the world after Carnival in Brazil – so they say. It's a ten-day party.

There is the opening ceremony – not a boring speech with polite applause but a two-hour build-up in the Mosh pit at the best rock concert you ever went to. There wasn't any music but the young people were drinking Sangria and getting high on life. Singing, clapping, jumping, girls hoisted high to the shouts of the crowd, baring their breasts to a stream of Sangria.

The floor was wet from wine and littered with so many empty plastic bottles that it was hard to stand. Wild, wild exuberance and we were right in the middle of it.

I'd never done anything like this before – in my normal life I wouldn't even have considered it; I was experiencing the world in a totally new way – the freedom, the abandon. That day I let myself go with it, a teenager again. I laughed, drank and sang with thousands of people: strangers and friends at the same time.

The pushing got much stronger. Girls were the worst, using all their weight. Breasts and buttocks pressed into me, the young women concerned had no interest other than to stand their ground in the square. It was an intense physical experience for someone like me, not used to touching people, especially strangers.

A group of guys started playing Human Dodgems with big smiles on their faces. I remember us shouting up to Vicky, our tour guide. She waved from a high balcony, five storeys up, amazed at where we were standing, in the eye of the maelstrom. She's 20 years younger than me, but I was the young person that day. I was right in the heart of it. That's exactly where I wanted to be at that moment – at the centre of life!

Finally it was time. A drum and a fanfare of horns introduced the rockets that officially opened proceedings. The thousands of eager festival goers in the square held up their red scarves and roared in salute. We were to wear those scarves from that point to the end of the festival. I wore mine for the rest of the trip. We were brothers and sisters together. Ticker tape streamed from balconies, the crowd went wild, inflatables bounced around the crowd. The noise, the excitement, the energy. It was life at fever pitch. I savoured these rare moments, like drinking the finest wine.

Ceremony over, we slid out of an exit, our clothes pink with sangria, pristine white no longer. We had a few beers up by the castle. A pretty brunette took photos of us as we sang *I can't take my eyes off you* to her with gusto. The impromptu parties continued, the old town completely packed with revellers.

Bull Run - Bring it On! Six guys totally free! It felt like we could do anything now.

We made our way to the start of the Bull Run course for the night-before briefing. There we learned the religion, history, the sequence of the run, and that there was no safe place on the course. Our guide gave us lots of advice like, "don't stand here" and "the bulls crash here" or "you wouldn't want to stand anywhere on this street, there is nowhere to hide". Bravado. A very Spanish term.

We finished the tour at a bronze statue of bulls trampling scared runners. It's larger than life and didn't faze me at all. I was ready to go. We were going to run tomorrow and listened to the "advice" of our guide; we earnestly discussed strategies for avoiding danger and completing the run. Our minds raced, revved with exciting anticipation and more.

That night we had dinner at a restaurant with an excellent view of the fireworks above the old citadel. Great fun, a huge cognac; dinner ended at 1am despite us knowing we had to be up at five. We didn't care, we were ready for anything.

I dressed in two t-shirts to guard against the cold of the piazza. We gathered two hours before the start, our choices becoming apparent when the tour group split: runners and watchers. Only five of us were running, the other forty watching.

God, I was so not here to watch! That's too much of how my life had been. I was there to live life's experience to the full.

Now we were ready; it was time.

Cleaning trucks were finishing clearing from last night. Squashed as we were, it wasn't easy getting out of the way. Crammed together, full of fear, adrenalin and Sangria, it didn't feel cold at all. I noticed many of the runners were much younger than us.

The watchers were escorted to balconies on the most dangerous parts of the course. It made me feel like we were the players on our own stage. This was real. This was happening. I was ready.

I can still hear the Catalan pipe and drum bands in the run up to the start. Nerves were building all around me. I started shifting from one foot to the other, but I had no thought of quitting. This Bull Run was meant for me, right here, right now.

The police manhandled us to create a corridor for the mayor and his party to inspect the course, randomly removing people as they went. I wondered why.

Finally the course was fully open. We walked down past our watching friends, who joked to us, but we didn't care. They were the watchers. Pah! I was focused, ready to go and although I saw my friends I hardly noticed what they said.

We took up our positions. Andy and Simon decided to stay in the square. Pete and I went up Estafeta street. We recognised the cameras on the way past and played it cool. Nothing like a bit more bravado before the main event.

There was nowhere to hide on the street except for a few shallow doorways. It was here we waited.

It starts ... The first rocket hasn't even been fired when a rush comes – it's an unmistakable sensation of thousands of people running without a sound. How could there be so much panic when they should know it's not yet time?

There's no danger. Not yet. We hold our ground.

The next rocket fires and the panic really starts. A young man stops in front of us, wide eyed and panting. He says, "It's the strays you have to watch!" but he's never run before, so how does he know? I'm amazed at how people have created stories without ever knowing the reality. Then he's gone as the next wave of panic starts. This one is real. Something is coming. We can sense it, no rocket signal required. We get ready.

And then they are here, the first group of bulls. Wow they are fast! Huge animals, tightly packed together. They rush towards us, full of power. We tense, we know what we are looking for now. Someone has already fallen and needs a medic. It's not the bulls but the people who are the danger!

As soon as the main group of bulls appear we take off, running fast with them. They are still faster. It's exhilarating – in that moment the strategies and the thinking all go out the window, it's just me and the bulls, I don't even notice the other runners. I know what to do. I just know.

When we stop running we are just outside the stadium, on a big high. Mission accomplished. A panting Pastores herder, following the bulls, stops by us. One cigarette too many maybe? I pat him on the back and ask him if it's over. He nods, unable to speak; over so soon.

We filed back to the Hemingway bar in the main square to check in, swapping stories, laughing, joking, triumphant. For two giant minutes that really was life at its best. When the thinking stopped we knew what to do. It was effortless. We were all safe, better than safe. We'd all had the time of our lives!

My lingering memory of that day was a young black bull that turned his head and looked me in the eye, before charging on up the course. So beautiful. Majestic. He was bred for this, to die this day; he was so noble. I hope he died well.

Now I know the run, I'm ready to go again and do it better. "Again, again, again", I hear the voice inside me cry, like a little kid. Now I know why people do it many times over many years, once they've run the first time. That was the first time I'd really experienced what I came to call my "best life": no thinking, no limits, just me experiencing life in the moment.

I had done it. I could do it. How could I take this feeling, this life back home with me? Now I wasn't worried about what would come next. I knew that just as I had known what to do for the bulls, I would know what to do in all the upcoming decisions and challenges in my life.

Leaving and Loving

Just as I had known exactly what to do the moment the bulls appeared in Pamplona, I knew that the next part of my journey was with B. I went home and packed my things.

This next phase of leaving my family was traumatic. I just kept putting one foot in front of the other, and it took me to Stourbridge, in the West Midlands, and to B.

This was a totally different world for me. All change. New people to get to know. New roads to drive and ride. New children to look after. Everyday life was very different, much simpler in some ways. No TV, we talked instead. Even what we ate was different, more nutritional. I loved our morning sessions spent making green smoothies. The energy and love that went into those drinks really made a difference in lots of ways.

I still went to London for meetings and my business continued, but it was a new train line, new views from the carriage windows and different logistics in planning my trip.

On the surface it was business as usual, but there was an undercurrent. My business partners were a bit nonplussed. They tried manfully to hide it, even though it was affecting them.

Change your location and everything seems magical as you discover ordinary things, places and situations for the first time. Burford Gardens; Ludlow Market and Castle were great excuses for riding fabulous roads and discovering great views; buying fresh produce and sampling local food; eating excellent fish and chips on the banks of the Severn River in Bewdley on a sunny summer's evening. Amazing coffee sharing a brown leather sofa in Boston Tea Party in Worcester. Going to the festivals at the Steiner school in Stourbridge.

Was it the locations or sharing those places and times with someone I was so close to? I rediscovered my childhood loves of Warhammer and painting figurines. It was all wonderful.

Looking back, I could have chosen the glamorous Caribbean, but no, it was Stourbridge. Stourbridge and B. In the simplicity of being her new partner I discovered a sharing and an intimacy that I hadn't had before in my life – or maybe it was so long ago that the memory had faded.

But how could such a feeling fade? Impossible! We were both on our journey together, revelling in our discoveries and relishing the joy of each other. Suddenly I had the most beautiful life. In those times I could see that all my businesses and all my striving for success meant nothing when you could live like this.

Business was important, money had to be earned and there was fun to be had, but where it had defined me for many, many years, it now took second or third place. I'd never felt like that before. It felt so right! I felt whole and complete. I was, and still am, so thankful for those times, the best of times.

After my mum died I'd been in denial and hadn't felt her loss. Oh, my world took a tilt, but I hadn't felt the full strength of it. B was so strong a woman that she levelled my playing field once more. That was huge for me.

I took a few pieces of original art to Stourbridge, ones that hadn't been hung before. They seemed to fit in my new place. One in particular was a small stormy seascape I'd bought to make a donation to McMillan Cancer Research in memory of my mum. It seemed to shine on the upstairs landing, in that unique way the sea can shine through a storm. It was a perfect reflection of our space.

I introduced B to bikes, too. I remember so clearly how nervous she was on the back of my big Harley, and how quickly her nerves turned into exhilaration in the same journey. It turned out that she was as passionate about riding as I was. Could it get any better than this?

There was a downside. My family really struggled with me and I with them. Relationships were broken or misplaced. In some cases everything seemed lost. In others we tried to keep things together, but it was not easy. My family had always been important to me, and I didn't know how this was going to work out. Deep down it worried me, but it seemed a price I had to pay there and then for being in such a wonderful place myself and experiencing a relationship like I'd never known before.

All the change meant nothing compared to this new life. As Mum would have said, sometimes you need to take a step back to take a couple forward. I was sure that was what was happening now. I was certainly caught up in the dance of life right then and I just went with it, trusting my compass, not knowing where it was taking me, but going anyway.

Old and New

And so my life was subtly changing, I was sailing to a new destination, the next step along the way.

I felt I was leaving familiarity, some beautiful places and people, and it was like leaving port – but I was drawn to go. The future beckoned. I would always treasure the experiences and the memories from my old life. It had nourished, developed, supported, exhilarated – frustrated and depressed me, too, in equal measure. Now was the time go back to the sea. I'd been away too long.

I know my boat well – it's me – so it will be with me all my life. Sometimes I know it too well, but when you are at sea there are always new things to discover. Even so, I have the skills and experience. I was confident and sure about travelling. I had new companions; some old ones I knew I would miss, but I was ready – ready to discover a new world. As my boat left the safety of the harbour we raised sails, feeling the wind, waves and the warm sunshine. I delighted to be at sea again. We were on our way.

I knew I could always come back to visit that familiar place. It would still be here, I was sure. Just then we were headed somewhere else and, just like when you leave port, for some hours we could see the land we had left getting hazy, receding, and then finally disappearing over the horizon line. Gone, but not forgotten. Never forgotten.

Now we are in open water. Alone with nature. What will it bring? Big waves or calm seas? A blind tanker storming across our path for us to take evasive action? Maybe a whale will come to eye us up, sitting a few feet from our hull and cruising with us before disappearing into the deep. Yes, the sea holds many secrets, many opportunities.

And still we hold to our course. I'm certain in my navigation; our destination will appear over the horizon ahead. I check the course and the sails. The boat feels good as the bow cuts the water, surf and spume cresting the sides and spraying us like young children having a water fight.

The waves start getting really big as we enter deep water, some of them much bigger than the boat! It looks like we will be engulfed, but no, every one slides underneath us and we tap their huge power, changing our direction slightly to surf off their heights. Wow, what a ride!

Then the universe tries to catch me out. There is always something. A rope that gets caught or we run out of diesel when we are motoring. Maybe some destinations we weren't expecting appear over the horizon. I hold to my course. I deal with whatever comes, calm, clear, knowing we have what it takes to be safe. I never doubt that we will make it safe to our next harbour. Together we have the confidence and the skills.

It feels so good to have that camaraderie on board, that sharing of fantastic surprises and dangers. We've come through it all together and that creates a special bond between us. More than friendship, it's something we'll have for the rest of our lives. We know we can rely on each other in those moments – good and bad.

There was a time, when I was new to sailing, we were on a night crossing to Martinique and I was off watch for the first time. Down below, trying to sleep, the boat started to roll and buck. Now that's a wakeup call! I rushed up into the cockpit, scared and disoriented. Later I would know that we were just passing the headland of St Lucia, where the Atlantic meets the Caribbean Sea. In twenty minutes it would be all over. I sat in the cockpit, helpless, wondering what was going on.

Eventually I fell asleep right there, to awake a few hours later in the bright light of a full moon reflected from calm waters. It was bliss. The sea gave me a rough ride and then showed me its beauty. Nowadays I see the beauty in all of the aspects of the sea, even though some might be challenging. Just like life, really.

And then a destination appears, indistinct at first. We adjust our course slightly to head there and we strain to see what the new land looks like. It is a world of possibility. I have no expectation of what it will bring, but I know it's going to be good.

First, it will be good to take the sails down and moor safely behind a new breakwater, that wall so strong it easily keeps out the power of the sea and provides a glassy smooth surface for the boat to glide to a stop. Then we can go discovering ...

Only a few steps from the boat, the harbour has wonders to offer me. A coffee shop or a bar. A grocery store selling produce I've never seen before. The fantastic faces of ordinary people living their own lives, in a way that is so different to the way I live mine.

Even the mundane things seem special because they are familiar things done differently. Then you branch out, explore some more, and even more amazing things await. It could be an old Roman fort, hot and cold volcanic springs, or some unbelievable local restaurant serving the most wonderful food – so cheaply, too. These are the things I live for, except it's really about me and my companions. It's about doing it together.

Our fantastic journey. We'll explore things here, savour and enjoy things and then a time will come to move on. The new becomes not new any more. It becomes the old. The cycle turns once more.

We'll know when that is and moving on will be great, too, knowing what we've learned and achieved and what excitement still lies ahead.

When I started my one of my business ventures, there was a guy who wanted to come with us and was happy to step aboard the boat before it left; but as the boat started to leave he stepped ashore. I don't know why, because he really wanted to leave his old life behind.

I tried hard to get him on board, but day by day the gap between the boat and the shore got bigger until we couldn't bridge it. Sad for both of us, an opportunity missed. Sometimes your companions leave you; their way is a different way. I should be fine with that, but I really want the best for them. It's like being a parent: you feel responsible somehow and yet you need to let them be themselves. Only they know what is their path. Let them choose. I'm sad when I see people go, but I found out from this experience that is better for all of us if they move on – and I do, too.

I stayed in one place for so long. It was a great place. I loved its familiarity, found many ways to enjoy that one location. I lived with great companions, and loved them, too. Sometimes there are good reasons to stay in one place; but something called me and I had to go – go where? I didn't know. I only knew the excitement of the journey. As I journeyed on, great things unfolded. Why wouldn't I want that? Sometimes it felt like I shouldn't have left. Familiarity is so comfortable, easy. Then I saw the sea, and I knew what I wanted: sunshine, waves, gulls and the wheel of a boat under my hand once more. Even though I hadn't been on a sailing vacation for years, I knew that feeling every day now.

Busy minded

Sometimes part of the hero's journey is losing your way, and having to find it again.

6.10 am. My mind is stirring, things to do today, problems carried over from yesterday, worrying at little nagging issues, how could I solve them? Time pressure mounting, got to get the day started, but not yet!

The sky is slowly turning from that deep magenta of the early hours, tinged with the orange flare of street lighting, to a warm grey. Will it be a nice day? The world isn't ready to share this secret quite yet.

My thoughts rove farther still, out to the future, things yet to happen – not possibilities, but rather outcomes I am pushing for. More worrying, niggling, controlling clouds my mind. Then I ponder my history and what it all means to me now, the way I do or don't do things, successes and mistakes, "am I enough?"

And I lie under a warm duvet in the warm embrace of my lover. We are together in that safe, quiet place that is unique to this part of the day. Talking, nuzzling, kissing, warm and comfortable in each other's arms. How can we make this beautiful time last longer? This tranquil place.

It's then I notice the blue sky. The secret has unfolded and it's going to be a beautiful day. I see that this beautiful space doesn't have to end with rising. We can keep this love, this safety, this warm feeling about life and take it with us into the day ahead.

No time pressure, no worry, enjoying all that is in the world around us. Why not take that time to be free?

I fought hard to try to hang onto the me that I had been on the road trip. Engulfed by all of the activity around me, pressure seemed to have returned. I'd left to start my journey, but now I was back, my old life seemed to be creeping in to take me back. My business seemed like a struggle and I didn't know why. I had two clients who leant on me, hard. They rang all the time, upsetting the joy of life that was supposed to be mine.

I felt I had to continue working with them. My business partners felt a separation and had their own views about my new life, which seemed to colour our work together. And that colour was grey. Not good. I had to work at it and make it right. That's what all my old conditioning told me was the way. Now I had two families to support and I was damn well going to do it.

Where was the wisdom of the Bull Run? Where was the freedom of the open road now? It seemed to be getting harder to find. I could get there, but each time it felt like a struggle of will.

The Tranquil Gardens

From the hustle of New York City to the bull run and the revellers of Saint Fermin I found myself blessed to be walking the long borders of the gardens at Dartington Hall, near Totnes in Devon, later that summer. The purple blue of the flowering agapanthus, the huge white poppy flowers, the yellow clematis, gracefully climbing a wall. They created an unmatched beauty and spoke to hours of dedicated love and care by the gardeners. I truly welcomed it into my life.

In caring for Lucy, it was in my mind to treat her gently; so I'd invited her along. I knew this was a great place and maybe we could both benefit. How wrong I was. For us it was a weekend of discord and struggle, when the intention was for harmony and calm. It seemed this magical place couldn't overcome the basic truth that was there for us right then.

Despite the turmoil between us, I found rest and calm within myself in the garden. I wondered at the perfection that was here in this magical valley, hidden from the outside world, a haven of peace.

I walked the paths and the grassy avenues. Each opened up a brand new vista of trees or sculpture. Each turn was a delightful surprise, thoughtfully designed, simply done and lovingly cared for. It took my breath away. I thought I must be in heaven.

Was the tranquillity in the sculpture of a reclining woman by the line of twisted horse chestnut trees? Or the pond and fern beds by the necking swans fountain? Maybe the architecture of the open air theatre with its grassy banks and carefully positioned, geometrically trimmed hedges. The giant gunnera plants were astounding, too, their size larger than life. This place was so complete, whole; it was perfect, and I'm sure that if I go back there now it will be just the same. It will have the same amount of love and care lavished upon it and it will be waiting to share its gifts with me.

There were little thatched garden houses, too, on a spiral pathway up one side of the valley. Positioned just so. Surrounded by flowers and plants, My little camera couldn't do it justice, but I took the photos anyway. So much beauty!

In each place there were the seating areas, all carefully positioned with a beautiful view and constructed to be slightly secluded, so that you could be alone with the garden even when there were other people there. I was so grateful to them for finding such perfect ways for me to enjoy this wonderful place. We found a wooden bench and stone wall, wrapped in soft hedging. It invited me to sit and presented a fantastic view, from the gigantic black wooden ball structure in the grass of the valley bottom, to a long and straight flagged staircase leading up the opposite side of the valley, surrounded by ornate trees, mature in all their glory. There were many spots like this. Take your pick ...

In this place I could breathe. Long, slow, comfortable breaths, drinking in the calmness and serenity of this place. Only the friendly chatter of the birds or the call of a passing gull intruded, but even they were part of the composition; like the very best music that connects with my emotions, fully and deeply. There are very few places I have ever been that give this gift. It's truly remarkable. I wanted my life to be like this always, not the mixture of intimacy and cacophony that I was experiencing. How could I have this in my life every day?

Then, as I relaxed even more, my eyes started to close and my thinking subsided. For a few moments I became part of the garden, totally calm and serene, a kind of tranquillity I have rarely known. Bliss. Lucy was right beside me, but even so close together physically, and as much as I cared for her, in that moment we were worlds apart.

I reached out, to be close to B and speak earnestly, even though she was far away. I communicated with quiet words, softly. With my love.

In those moments, I seemed to almost leave my body and fly up into the tops of the tallest trees, where the wind rustled the leaves and branches to say that rain was on the way. The grey clouds turned to mist and the garden became bathed in a pleasant dewy damp. The grass seemed pleased to be wetted and turned an even more lush shade of green. Then rain started to fall in earnest, a seaside summer shower, with the sun pushing to peep through the cloud, giving me a welcome sense of warmth. Rain and sun, both at the same time. Perfect. The seat was sheltered enough to allow me to watch the rain as it swept through the valley like a friendly blanket. Nature had truly arrived to bless man's husbandry in this bountiful place.

It didn't feel cold, even when the rain started getting heavier, with drops falling from the hedging that had protected me up to now. I marvelled at the delicacy as the water touched my skin.

Somehow it seemed to make my experience of this garden, of life, complete in that moment. I couldn't ask for more.

In due course, at the right moment, the rain subsided and it felt like time to go. Up the spiral path, past statues of a donkey and a ball of more spirals, a gateway in the yew hedge appeared, to let me out. I was not sad to leave, more satisfied by having been there and oh, so grateful to have spent my time in this wonderful place. This was a different space for me. It wasn't often that I'd allowed myself to really drink in the beauty of the world in this way.

It was something like my road trip. It was about allowing myself to see the world and not be so caught up with me. That was something I could do more of. Maybe I could take Dartington Gardens with me in my heart and mind and be in that space whenever I wished ... The designers and keepers of that beautiful place had made it easy for me with their great gift. I intended to use it as often as I could.

Fast and Slow

Back in London a few days later I met a man living very fast. People were crowding round him, all of them wanting him to go somewhere, do something or meet someone. They were all "beautiful people", too. You know what I mean: well dressed and well appointed, successful business men and adoring women – he was the Usain Bolt of business.

Surely he should have been on top of the world? Isn't this what everyone aspires to? He's rich, lives in Monaco, earns more in a month than most of us do in ten years. Wouldn't you want that? Think what life would be like if you could go out tomorrow and buy a helicopter or a Lamborghini just because you fancied it! I heard he did just that.

And yet he was living so fast that his face was grey and his eyes were pinpoints. In fact, thinking about it, maybe he was on drugs? Quite possibly. Who knows? Some people do anything to keep up a fast pace. All he seemed to want to do was to go somewhere and rest. Maybe it was because he'd been up late last night, playing just as hard as he worked. When I talked to him he could hardly hear me. He made up some vague comment in reply that showed he wasn't really listening. Maybe he wasn't Usain Bolt after all? UB breaks the world record and still has time to do a lap for his fans and dedicate the race to his mum! Somehow I didn't think our fast and successful man would be doing that.

It didn't make sense to me. And then it did. I reacted so strongly to him because his pain was so familiar. I'd lived that life. Going fast. Too fast.

Going to London next week. Got to pack in five meetings to make the day a successful one. Arriving home too late for dinner, but eating it anyway, watching an hour of telly, but not really watching. Going to bed without a cuddle or any kind of meaningful conversation with my so-called loved ones. Eating, drinking and sleeping in another world – a world of my own where my thoughts were trying to keep up with everything that I was doing and everything everyone else needed me to do, yesterday!

In that fast life, my old life, this continued seven days a week, in the weekend just replacing business meetings with standing on the touchline for my son or watching my daughter ride. Even walking the dogs was often spent on the phone, somewhere else.

It reached the stage where I couldn't sleep. I would wake up every two hours each night and beat off the thoughts of all the things to do the next day, thoughts that were an attempt to get the next day off to a quick start. Like a sprinter getting off the blocks, we are all trying to beat the 100m world record every day – only Usain B breezes it while we all struggle.

This week, in particular, I'd slowed down. I had got up and had breakfast with B and the family. On purpose. I'd done my tai chi to clear the brain and get my energy activated. "All very hippie", I hear you cry, but why not have all my resources to help me with the day? Don't the sprinters get themselves prepared for their race? I deliberately didn't open my email until 10 am.

Now, when I open my computer each day to do some work, my plan is to keep it simple, and just focus on two things to do in that day; and then I see my inbox. I always seem to have fifteen things to do before I can get to the two things that are actually important to me.

I used to look at my mail before I got up – the disadvantage of mobile computing. My phone would start ringing, too, more interruptions, some things very worthy – my kids for example – but also a bunch of calls to do things for other people when I was trying to JUST GET MY TWO THINGS DONE!

But I know it wasn't about the two things I wanted to get done or the fifteen things that cropped up along the way, it was how I reacted to them. I missed opportunities to enjoy life a bit more, to be with my kids, my dogs, the wonderful world out there – that Dartington Garden feeling that was open to me all the time. I was so wrapped up in other things that I was missing it. Business, duty and money were pushing themselves back to the top of my agenda. What did that do to the peace and joy I had found putting life and living first? It certainly wasn't living the dream as far as I was concerned.

I started switching my phone off in the evening. Sprinters get a good night's sleep, why shouldn't I? It's another part of being good and ready for the race. In my busy life I'd struggled to sleep well. Then I dragged myself into the day and did the best I could. I wanted to have the chance for every day to be a "personal best", yet like the Fast Man I wasn't letting myself be in my best shape. That was going to change, I thought; but try as I might I still thought that working hard and staying focused was the way. Yes, being that Fast Man was what I was trained to be, a habit that I was very familiar with. It was the rut I was in, I thought.

How could I change that? I struggled. I tried different ways to organise my life. It wasn't working. It had to work! It had to work NOW! I didn't want to be the Fast Man.

The ultimate test for me was going on holiday. How often have you crammed so much in before you go that you haven't packed a bag, or even thought about leaving, or got excited about the prospect, until late on the evening of the night before the flight? Did you get to the point where you were cursing booking the blasted holiday in the first place?

Well, the good news is that you get to take the holiday anyway, almost falling onto the plane. From the moment I strap on my seatbelt I know the party has started and everything changes. Don't you feel great when you are there? I do – most of the time. One thing I noticed is that the first couple of days I feel very tired, feel ill even as my body finally relaxes after 120 consecutive 100m race days. That's my body telling me something. I wonder why I never listened.

When my wrapped-up, absorbed life was really getting to me, I even managed to not enjoy the break because I'd brought the thinking of all that work and pressure with me. How I wasted those holidays. That was really being the Fast Man, having luxury and not enjoying it. Fortunately that didn't happen to me often, but I'd noticed it was happening more and more. When I allowed myself to have a holiday from "that" life and I really got to relax, feel great, enjoy the family and the beauty of the place I was visiting, it was so different. Talk about recharging the batteries! Why couldn't every day be like that? Even when I wasn't on vacation?

When was the last time you did some great work in a day and had time to enjoy life, too? You don't need to be a Buddhist monk to get this – or Usain Bolt even! I'm just an ordinary guy, and I was getting a glimpse of something new, a new way to live. I thought to myself, 'I just have to get out of my old habits first'. And there was the rub. The more I tried, the more the life I wanted seemed to elude me. Looking back it's so obvious what was happening.

I used to travel on the train a lot, and when I did get a seat I would get a computer out and work. Even when I had to stand I would be thinking about what I should do next. I was urgently trying to keep up with the to-do list and losing. There was no space in my life. No space at all! However hard I tried.

And then I moved house and changed my train journey, and without even trying anything new, that created an opportunity. I started writing.

I had always thought that I would write my book in a special place. I even found the perfect location, on a game reserve in Africa. If only I could take six weeks to go and sit on a veranda overlooking the game trails and write, I thought; that would be fantastic. Of course it was never going to happen in the world I was inhabiting then, but the 8.23 from Stourbridge to London Marylebone became my place. That accidental space was a godsend for me.

The phone didn't work because of the patchy signal. No interruptions, fantastic! There was wifi, but I knew that my email, those fifteen things, would just come and find me, so I stayed away. Instead, I wrote and it was magical. Everyone has a book in them, they say, and this was going to be mine. Trip by trip it built. No pressure or stress, just quality time. Me and my keyboard – lovely.

I didn't set out to write a book. I didn't even know what I was writing about, but each journey was a vacation for me. Soon I started to know what I was going to write even before I got on the train. I would sit down, open my iPad and the words would flow. I would disappear from the busy world to another place. Now, you could say that I was still wrapped up and absorbed, and I'd agree with you − but I was looking in a different direction. When I was in this place I felt totally at peace, relaxed and − dare I say it − inspired; a totally different type of absorption.

In one sense, my road trip and running with the bulls was just a holiday, the mood of it quickly forgotten once I was back. Meeting the Fast Man was a great reminder that I wasn't going to be like that any more. Now with my writing I had found one way to bring life that wasn't just escaping from my circumstance, it wasn't like packing my sailing bag. When I was writing I was still in my normal world, I was just seeing it differently.

And what about our grey, fast man? There was a big word hidden in his story: Success.

Is he successful? According to most, possibly; he would certainly be admired, envied even. Once upon a time I would have loved to be like him. Was I successful? I had been caught trying to live up to expectations − my own, and what I thought everyone else needed from me, too. I was always striving for more. Success was a hard taskmaster for me.

That was something I needed to let go of; I needed to find a new way. Generally it seemed to be all about money, but suddenly I realised that time was really important to me. I mean quality time, but you've probably guessed that. What's the point in having lots of money if you've got no time. Headspace, time to be really clear and enjoy life. That was important to me. I realised real riches didn't belong in the bank.

My train journey and my writing was a big clue. Trying hard to fix my life wasn't what would get me there – but I so wanted to fix things. Writing had nothing to do with solving a problem, fixing something; in fact I had no idea where my writing was leading, but I was curious about that – and it felt good.

There was a clue in here for me. When I tried to fix and control things, that's when it all seemed like hard work. When I went with my instinct, my compass, it was beautifully simple.

My Urban Park Bench

My urban park bench
Sits high on a hill amidst the mown park lawns
Old, worn and marked
It shares the world with me again

The blooming horse chestnuts
Shading bluebells and cow parsley
The birds sing merrily on their business
And the squirrels laugh at the dog's failed chase

A refuge in the midst of suburbia
A place of calmness and beauty
It greets me quietly
And invites me to rest a while

I look up to the hills
Bathed in sun or masked in cloud
The crowded houses beneath
While my Labrador waits patiently

It's always there for me
Whether I notice or not
The park bench always has time
Peace and a wonderful view

B and I lived a beautifully simple life in those days. Walking the dog each morning, chatting with friends and each other. Whether it was dull or fine, there was a magic at Mary Stevens Park in Stourbridge that was always there for us.

The church bells played to us on a Sunday morning as the day peeked in through the window of our bedroom. It wasn't all pressure and strife – far from it. It started with that dog walk in a wonderful Victorian park, full of magnolias, beautifully planted beds and a pond for the birds.

Oh, and did I tell you about the illicit thrills of the ice cream van? I always joked with the pretty girl serving us about her fictitious holiday in the Caribbean. She wished!

I will always remember those times – the best of times. Full of love, sharing and optimism for the future. Life couldn't be better. As I close my eyes now I can see the view of the skyline from that bench; I can feel how great that part of my life was. The sun was shining brightly in my heart.

Ed Sheeran's song *This* was playing inside me.

Downtime

Are you driven? Do you wake up every day with a list of things to do already on your mind? Do you feel stressed the moment you open your eyes and look at the clock? Is that the time!

I did that in my old life. It had been creeping back into my life and even now I still get caught up in it occasionally.

It may seem like a small thing, but for me it was one of my major trials, continuing to follow the new path, my newly found inner compass, when the way I had done things in the past had, on the surface, worked so well. I had been successful in business, in making money. Now I had two families to support, the temptation to go back to the old way was just too strong. I did it, when I should have known better.

In the old days, every day I had to get up for the train, my calendar solidly booked with meetings. Or maybe I had to catch a flight for a client visit. Even after my corporate life I still had deadlines. I worked with a number of collaborators around the world, with early morning and late night calls. It was a time when my weekends were just as busy, and being the "taxi service" for my kids and their busyness made me even busier! Of course I wanted to be with them, but ...

My only real glimpse of respite was walking the dog, even though I didn't seem to see what was right in front of me. She always loved the company. Even when I wasn't present because I was on the phone, she always came to me with a doggy smile and a waggy tale. It took me a long time to get what she was telling me: slow down, be with me, right here, right now. Isn't nature beautiful? Isn't this fun?

I was caught in my thinking. I didn't live in the world. I lived in my mind and it told me to go go go. Time is money and it's wasting! Feeling responsible for so many people, I filled my time and rushed from thing to thing. A great day was when I packed even more stuff into an already busy schedule, just so I didn't let anyone down. It came to the point where I felt guilty if I had some time off! Where had my beautiful life gone to?

At that time, life felt like one of those sixteen-piece puzzles – you know, the ones where the pieces are in a frame and there is one space left free so you can move the pieces around to reveal a picture. You spend a lot of time messing around with the pieces trying to rearrange them. You think it through, try something intelligent and the pieces are farther away from finished than ever! So you do more, moving faster and faster, trying harder to get it done. Well that's the way I did it.

Isn't that a bit like life when you are busy busy busy? And what would happen if on top of all this busyness and thinking, the last slot, the free slot was filled by an actual piece? You see it's actually a fifteen-piece puzzle and it only works with a free slot. That empty space is vital, without it nothing else works. Yet how many of us fill that space? I'm pretty sure I did.

My mobile phone, Facebook and the internet, email. They were the sixteenth piece and maybe the seventeenth, too. Does that make it easier to get the job done? If life truly were this puzzle it would make finishing it impossible, wouldn't it? And that's exactly how it felt to me. I'd become trapped in a puzzle that I just couldn't finish!

(The Dean of Harvard business school talked about the sixteen-piece puzzle in an open letter to undergrads that has become very famous. If you've never heard of it, Google, and have a read. It's well worth it.)

Where had my best life gone now? How about love, intimacy or just plain enjoying life?

Some of our best times, our most creative moments, our inspiration, come when or after we give ourselves permission to relax and slow down – you know, that moment when you actually let yourself really enjoy the lie in and suddenly you know exactly what to do, or that long hot soak or even that glass of wine accompanied by laughter and friendship. How different is that compared with worrying on your own about how things are going to turn out and getting on the phone to people to try and make something happen – again?

I started to call it downtime and schedule it regularly, and then noticed how hard I was finding it to keep that appointment. The guilt made me uncomfortable. At least now when I sacrificed it to fit in that little extra item that someone wanted me to do, I realised what I was doing.

When I did – often accidentally – take a break, some great moment of creativity would arrive to remind me that the sixteenth piece, of space and freedom, is vitally important.

I used to have a great boss, a guy named Julian Eames, whom I really admired. He wandered round his business saying "work smart, not hard" – and this was in a business where work hard play hard was the way. Of course, working hard was, and is, an easy option. It's easy to feel the effort, like it makes a difference.

In Julian E's business, people worked hard to bring in the big deal at the eleventh hour of the deadline and got big kudos for it from their peers. What Julian really loved, and the basis for his lasting success, was people who had their number sorted before the month even started and had plenty of time to think how to be even smarter.

Now I was trapped in a classic case of "Do as I say and not as I do". I knew that I was doing wrong, but I did it anyway! If I've told you that bikes are my vice in a gentle sort of way, then this was my hard core addiction and I was heading for trouble.

I was living this way with the best of intentions: wanting to succeed, wanting to provide, wanting to be good, trying hard to make it all work. I got deeper and deeper in and I couldn't seem to shake it.

Soaring

Birds have been prominent in my life. Let me start with a little picture of a peregrine falcon that my brother bought many years ago, by a respected painter called Norman Orr.

As I understand it, Orr only painted birds of prey. The peregrine is a little bird. Proud and attentive, feathers slightly ruffled, it watched over my mother in her bedroom for years. It was a comfort for her and is a comfort for me in my bedroom now she's gone. I took that picture with me to each new place. It was a guardian, calm, assured and knowing. It hung over my bed and I knew I was safe. A good feeling has always accompanied that image.

How do these feelings happen? Are they just rampant sentimentalism on my part? I don't think so. They aren't planned, they just seem to arrive in my life and I notice them. Sometimes they are big WOW moments that strongly punctuate my life. Sometimes I don't notice them at the time, like the peregrine, but then later they come to mind and I realise a significance that I hadn't seen before. It's life happening for me, in and around me, to me. It's the part that I play in this huge production called the universe, a great chance for me to really experience life. I always hope to play my part and meet life with open arms as much as possible.

I first found Norman Orr at a hotel we used to stay at in Scotland in my childhood. I used to love sitting back in a big leather chair, in front of a roaring fire and read a really good book. I would have just come in from the cold and the contrast was fabulous. Warm, safe, and exciting, too, lost in an entertaining narrative.

I'd stay there for hours, engrossed in my reading and I'd be sitting beneath something really special: *The Eagle* painting, by Norman Orr. It must have been twenty feet high and similarly wide; really imposing. The subject was a huge golden eagle bringing a sheep back to the eyrie. Massive, larger than life, a symbol of power and majesty. It remains strong in my memory to this day, an anchor to that warm fire and engaging reading.

Then, a few years ago, when I was on another bike road trip to the Isle of Skye, I met the eagle again. We were riding back from the Talisker Whiskey Distillery, on a spit of land in the north west of the island, and just as we came back to the main road a big sea eagle flew over our heads, maybe only twenty feet away. It was totally breathtaking to be so close to such a wonderful creature. I'll bet he was on his way back to his eyrie, too ...

To top that, on the way home we visited the hotel with the Norman Orr painting. It's in Dunkeld, Perthshire. We stopped there and although it's now part of a big chain of hotels, a lot of the old place was much the same, including the eagle picture.

On the way out of Dunkeld we passed over the Tay bridge, a big stone arch, and just then an osprey dived down beside us to fish in the river. Ospreys were almost extinct in Scotland when I was a kid, but they are coming back now. Again, a wonderful bird had passed within a few feet of us.

All these experiences seem to "join the dots" of my life. They chart my course amongst the cacophony, the busyness and the struggling that has been large in my life experience. They show me that there is a bigger picture. They gave me a glimpse of the real me, even when I was lost in my addiction. I never used to believe in this whole "universe" thing. String theory? An invention of some brilliant scientists and mathematicians, I thought – all far beyond my ken, as they say in Scotland. Beyond understanding. Now I see evidence in my own life that there is some pattern to it. A pattern that I sometimes get to discern.

This reminds me of the time I was riding with the Harley crowd over the Picos Mountains in Spain – and I mean right over! We were meant to take the tunnel lower down, but it was closed for repairs. So over the top we went, up where snow poles line both sides of the road to show where to drive in wintertime. Somewhere near the top we rounded a bend to discover a flock of vultures circling low over the road ahead. We rode right underneath them. Circling, riding on the updrafts, separate and together, individuals with a common purpose. There were hundreds of them. I found out later they were on their way to Africa and it's quite normal. For me it was an unbelievable feeling, just being there with them. I was really living in that day: I planned nothing, did nothing to make it happen – it just happened. It's always like that. Life opens doors – all you have to do is walk through them; oh, and maybe put yourself in a place to see them in the first place.

What do these chance meetings with these great birds mean in my life? It seems that at certain times, when life is truly unfolding for me, raptors appear. They are always special to me. A good omen, flying high and proud, harnessing the natural energies of the wind to propel themselves to the skies.

At one point in my life I wanted to own a bird, to tame it, to train it, but nowadays I see them flying free and high, and I know that that's how things are meant to be, for them and for me.

Today I feel the wind beneath my wings more often; I feel the power of the updraft, and I know that I have that power and majesty in me. It fills me to the point where I feel I can do anything, be anything and yet it's just me, only me. When I feel like this, that's when I know life is unfolding for me, and I am really letting it in. It's when the seemingly unlikely and uncalled for things happen to surprise and delight that I know I'm there. It's then that I really experience life. Is it possible to feel this every day? If being "driven" was my addiction, these great experiences were signs sent to me to remember the true path, I'm sure of it.

These beautiful birds were showing me that just when you don't plan life, when you put off the blinkers that come with focusing on specific objectives or goals, that's when the unexpected arrives. I understood that intellectually, and I'd experienced what life was like when I just let it happen, but my default setting seemed to be to plan and control, fix the problems and focus on the outcomes. After thirty years of living that way it was ingrained in my approach to life, even when I had seen how life could be so much better done another way.

Monday Morning Thinking

This is something that happened to me every week, without fail, for many years. Some people would say it's getting ready for the game, others that it's performance anxiety. For me it was more like counting all the baggage I carried with me and putting myself under pressure when there was never any need for it. Surely this was my new life, everything should be an amazing adventure by now?

Its 8:46 a.m. and I'm past that point – for this week. Every Sunday I'm chilled, happy, enjoying my day and then some time before 6 a.m. I wake up and start thinking ...

... about work

... about life

... about things that have happened and not happened

... about things that could happen ...

It leaves me with a sense of dread, not a good feeling, about the week to come.

I know now how life can be, how things can flow when I follow my inner compass, so I look for a way to feel better. I ditch my logical thinking. Let's look at all the positive things that happened last week: a great step forward with a business project; a great ride on a bike. No, that didn't help. With the pressures of goals and achievement on my shoulders, fear and worry are back, I've fallen back into the old habit of being driven.

So I try to do something simple, like look outside to see if the weather is going to be good or listen to the birdsong and try to enjoy the beauty and simplicity of it all. Somehow that doesn't cut it either.

I get up. I put on some workout clothes and get on the exercise bike, cycling away to the sound of the Eagles and *Hotel California* on shuffle. I so want it to be *Wasted Time*, but instead my iPhone gives me *Victim of Love*, with its slow driving beat. The pedals whirr round in time to the music.

And magically, as I pedal to the music, the feeling goes.

The day seems sunnier. I am ready. The week will unfold, maybe not as I planned it, but with added twists and turns. There will be sunshine and rain, but we'll be out there enjoying the weather for the freshness and beauty it brings.

Funny how this happens every Monday? Is it like that for other people, too? Although B has never experienced it – lucky her. A little person in our house is experiencing it, too. He doesn't do it every Monday like me, but he's doing it today. Making himself ill, albeit mock ill, at the thought of something. Maybe it's the ridicule of his friends over his new short haircut. Something that would be small for me, but for him seems huge, enough to want to be sick and stay off school. As if a day will make a difference. Still, it shows it's not just me! Anyone can get it.

B has some great advice: don't believe those thoughts.

She's so right. You are just one thought away from greatness. Every single thought, if you just change one of them, just slightly, leads to great things. Wonderful things. That's how life should be – is – so don't resist it, just enjoy what comes to you. It's all as it is meant to be.

Sometimes my Monday morning thinking had been much worse than this; it seemed to be getting better. The interesting thing is, I could have just stopped having these sessions, but somehow I was resisting, like the iceberg that was slowly crumbling into the sea. It was still there, still floating in my mind and it seemed so real to me, just once a week.

As the day and the week unfolded, the iceberg seemed to shimmer and disappear from sight like magic. Things would always be much better than I imagined them to be on those early Monday mornings. It was my weekly appointment with delusion. When would it finally shimmer to never reappear? I endured.

Different train, different day

Different train ... different day
Somehow things seem ... well ... different
It's not quite sunny,
But it is warm ... warm enough.

What happened yesterday?
I lost a thought on the motorway
Cruising at 70 mph into my future
A beautiful future

Where things might look uncertain
I paint them with possibility
Let life take its unfathomable course
And I'll take what it gives ... gratefully

No great plans or demands
What is there will be there anyway
A kind of western fatalism?
Loving what is ...

It's a perfect place
With friends and family
Travel and music
Business and pleasure together

Mr Blue Sky

One day, I don't quite remember when, I woke up with a calmness and peace that felt really good; and then it surprised me. Hold on, last night I couldn't stop thinking – thoughts that gathered round me like a dense fog, clouding my vision, making my head spin. They had faded to nothing but clear, cool, peaceful silence – apart from the early morning birdsong, that is.

I didn't think. Instead some things just came to me and I felt how right they were. It was like last night turned inside out. Then nothing seemed right. Now everything was clear.

I showered and dressed feeling good, looking good and ready for a great day. Next stop: friends, business, sunshine and another day in paradise.

Of course it didn't turn out quite like that. The friends played hard to get – I forgave them. Some technical problem I was working on whilst on the move wouldn't solve (I wonder why). The Apple store didn't have anything we needed in stock – but we could go back next week. The train was delayed going home; never mind.

Even the deal I'd just closed went a little awry with a couple of suppliers, but I got it back, even to the point of improving the margin over the original.

This was a place where everything was fun, everything was possible, business was a game, friends treasured. When you are in this place of clarity and wisdom, setbacks are brushed aside with a smile. Could it be like this every day, please?

When I am in my best life, it's a great place. I am unbeatable. That's why I wanted to be there every day. I so wanted that. I so wanted somebody to show me the way, the button to press, the technique to take me to that place.

B had been talking to me about "slowing down". She talked like everyone knows what it is – slowing down, I mean. Was it doing less? All my working life I'd been busy goal-seeking, achieving, working hard, and on the surface that had worked. This shift was one of the biggest trials on my hero's journey: how would I build something without doing what I'd always done, how would I build something by doing less? It couldn't be right, my thoughts told me. But somewhere deep down I felt the truth of it. And then, on that morning, I could see it, I could see the layers of my life.

I'd spent the weekend running from one vehicle to another, driving here, there and everywhere to get our activities to fit together. I was still doing it. I was late for a dinner engagement. I never used to be late. It's too much! Then I saw the layers: if I wasn't rushing around with vehicles I could walk the dogs. But walking the dogs meant missing the kids ...

In a slippery slope, one thing led to another and quality time disappeared completely from my days. When had I last done my tai chi or gone to the gym? Weren't they both important parts of balancing my mental activity with something physical? If it was important for me to be at my best then why was I ignoring them? I wasn't spending quality time with the people I love either. I spent time apart, thinking about them or just texting and emailing them. What was that about?

Come to think of it, how much time was I taking up on my phone, trying to make up for lost opportunity? Then all of a sudden the phone was part of the problem. Yet another thing sucking me away from life. I was getting the sense that less is more.

Being totally focused on one thing at a time would give me more quality and a better result. I needed to deal with interruptions better. They were disturbing and always added another piece of work onto the list, usually at the top. The seventeen-piece puzzle again!

At least now I could see how slower could be better. Time for loved ones. Time for pleasurable things like riding a bike in the sunshine. Time for quality work and a better result. I knew that this was the right way. I just didn't seem to be doing it! It felt like I was wishing I was living life one way while actually living it a totally different way.

Another trial, another challenge, to integrate what I was learning into all of life. I felt like the hero of one of those old slapstick comedy movies, one foot in the boat and one on the shore, and the boat is moving away.

Into the Clear Blue

As you can probably imagine, having read this far, I had been deep, deep in the turbulence of the changes in my life. I had a strong and ever-growing need to make a breakthrough in the way I was living, how I was being, into the clear air and simple living that beckoned beyond the turbulence, beyond the trials and tests.

There is a fantastic Chuck Yeager story, about his historic flight in the Bell XI aircraft, where he broke the Mach 1 barrier for the first time ever. The speed of sound. When I was a boy this was high tech. This was the sort of thing that a young man dreamt of.

Yeager was in a craft that was essentially a rocket engine guided by a man. A very brave man. Up until that point, some scientists believed that the sound barrier was a physical barrier; the design of the airplane lacked some key knowledge. Yeager pushed the limits, knowingly, and even though things got rough getting close to the sound barrier, he stuck with it. I'm sure he made light of it, like the great test pilot he was. Next thing, the Mach meter jumped off the scale and after the boom of the barrier the ride became smoother and the plane more flyable.

Just in case you want to know, Chuck Yeager retired a general, having lived and loved the dangerous life of a test pilot at the very edge of science. He said it was his duty, but I bet he lived for that life. On retiring he remarked, "All that I am, I owe to the Air Force".

"Great story," I hear you say, "but what's that got to do with changing, my journey, the search for a new me, transformation or whatever you want to call it?" Well, it's a great analogy for what was happening in my life.

At the start of my journey everything seemed quite natural. Ok, there were some significant events like leaving the home life I'd had for many years – that was leaving the mother ship for sure, but new experiences beckoned. I knew they were going to be so meaningful and I was eager for them. Bring it on! Like Chuck in the hot seat before the ride really kicked in.

Then things started to develop. My family and friends at large created the turbulence of not understanding, or maybe not even wanting to understand where I was coming from in my new way of being. All my business activities created turbulence, too. They were founded on the premises of my old life and just didn't seem to fit the emerging me. I was committed to them and I started to wrestle with them, trying to bend them in the new direction.

I created turbulence, too. I resisted my own changes like mad! Very strange, but true. The old me was so familiar: what I did, my way of being in the world. Basic things like my desire to support everyone else before me, being the good provider. Or working hard. I always told my kids that the one thing our family was good at was working hard. Hell, I'd worked six and a half day weeks, twelve hours a day for years – not so easy to get out of that habit – or so I thought.

So just like Chuck Yeager, I worked the controls of my life. I tried harder than ever to take control. That was stressful and a lot of effort, too. I'm not sure that anything Chuck did was any use, but he stuck with it even when he thought the plane might disintegrate or blow up! I doubt that anything I did was any use either. Maybe it was – it sure kept me busy, and focused, too. Maybe it even prolonged the agony. Agony? Yes, for me it was a painful time, but just like Chuck I got through it into the clear blue skies beyond. More of that in a moment. For now, I want to tell you just how it happened for me – it was amazing.

For years I'd had a vision of "getting the stars to line up". So many times I chased a situation that was so close to being perfect I could almost taste the satisfaction, the success that would be there at the end of the rainbow, when the stars lined up. Of course, the universe doesn't work to my command, pots of gold don't magically appear at the end of the rainbow. Well, that's not how I think it works. The stars don't line up just because I want them to, however much I wish for it. If the stars are going to line up it's not because of me, or for me either. The universe is just the universe. It turns and changes and we are all just the tiniest parts of it. How could I have ever expected it to do my bidding?

Yet in those turbulent times that is exactly what I was trying to do. Using all my knowledge and past experience I was "going to make this plane fly". Can you feel the stress in me? Boy, the beads of sweat trickled off my brow, I didn't sleep, I worried, and I stuck with it; it was my duty surely? It was tough.

And then ...

I started to realise, maybe not consciously, that when I stopped trying to control and fix everything there were some delicious moments of joy in my life. Music, for example. I hadn't played music for thirty years, but a £5 harmonica and free lessons from the wonderful J.P. Allen reintroduced some long-lost brightness to me. It was and is wonderful; I don't care what anyone else thinks about how I look and how my music sounds. I played in the queues at the Olympics in London. I played in après ski cafés in France. I played my harmonica walking the dog in the park. I even crashed an afternoon concert in Worcester UK playing the harmonica solo in a Bob Dylan song, sung by a great local guitarist. It was all great. It worked for me. Who knows where it's going to take me? I could be on stage sometime soon. I might even set that as a goal, but in reality as long as I'm playing and having fun, it's enough.

There were other things, too – seemingly inconsequential things from long ago, that did the same thing: strategy games, my beloved motorcycles and not least, my B.

I started painting, modelling and playing strategy games. I didn't need to compete, I just loved what I was doing, but even so, just doing it the way I wanted to, I came fourth in my first national tournament, without ever having thought of winning. Now, that's what I call success, doing it my way.

There were new things, too, like writing and video production. Writing led me to publishing this book. I never set out to write it, but it just seemed to be the natural thing to do. If this is my fifteen minutes of fame, as declared by Andy Warhol in the sixties, then I'm very happy with it. All joyous, all things that I can't stop myself doing, they are so much fun.

Where do they lead to? Surely you can't make a living doing that? What about your family? All those questions beckoned, but didn't need to be answered right then. My videos developed from a bit of fun, to marketing and building online products and finally to helping others put their own videos together. So there is money in it, enough to keep everything going and flowing. There's love and satisfaction in it, too, something I could hardly say about my life beforehand.

Like Chuck Yeager I looked up and around me, marvelling at the clear blue sky that surrounded me, seeing the stars above, clear and bright, enjoying the flight, the new way.

In moments like those, just like I think it happened to the great man, Yeager, the controls are quiet in my hands and there is no need to fight any more. There's nothing to do except trust in this new life. I don't think words can express those first few moments, but I really wanted you to know how special this feeling is. Maybe you are wondering how I can compare small life experiences with arguably one of the biggest events in the history of flight? Well, it was that big for me.

The fact that you were drawn to reading this means you are probably going through a change in your life. Or maybe you are considering it. It may not happen for you exactly as it happened for me. You may have little or no turbulence to ride out. Just know that you don't have to fight the controls, they will go quiet in your hands, and then before too long you will be glimpsing clear blue skies of your own. You don't have to be brave, it's all happening for you. Maybe the universe delivers that pot of gold right to your feet after all. It did for General Yeager, and for me, too.

Up with the birds – Coldplay, August 2012

Helen and I had started an occasional penchant for going to concerts – gigs – together. We had fun at Ed Sheeran at the Brixton Academy and I wanted to do more. I went online and bid on Coldplay tickets for the whole family. It was not cheap, but I didn't realise the magic that was about to unfold – priceless, as they say in the TV advert.

Then the day arrived. We'd recently been to the Olympics, not far away in London, but this was the event I'd been looking forward to, the family, together.

It was warm and sultry that day. We got to Emirates Stadium in London in the afternoon to take our seats and wait in anticipation. We chatted, strained, polite. There was some reticence, some distance between us. I hadn't noticed quite how much thinking went unsaid until those few hours. It felt wrong, unnatural, even. Not good.

Next to us was a family whose father had motor neurone disease and from being fully alive two years ago could hardly move. I was amazed at how much they were together as a family, despite his illness, or because of it.

In comparison I was fit and healthy, but we were nowhere near as present with life. That felt big.

The weather started to turn. The clouds came down and the temperature dropped. It rained. Suddenly we were as cold as the conversation. Lucy wasn't well at that time, and she hadn't brought another layer to wear. I couldn't let her stay for hours in the cold – I cared for her, after all; and in that moment I know that I did more than care, I loved her still. It was an uncomfortable realisation in that moment, to know that I wanted to be part of her solution when I was really part of her problem. How could I square that circle? It wasn't clear.

We left our seats to get her something, and found a t-shirt at a stall, one that she loved. It kept her warmer, too. Both of us were grateful for that. Even so, the politeness and the distance were palpable.

And then it came, the show, and boy, what a show! We were lost in the performance, and pretty soon we were transported by our favourite songs – songs we shared as a family.

We marvelled at the fireworks, the inflatables, the light show and the videos, but above all, it was the music, the feelings. As we waved our wristband lights to the songs, we even became part of the performance together. This was heaven, our little moment.

As I looked round, everyone was smiling, laughing, dancing, lost in the music like revellers, our barriers dropped in self-expression. We were together like we hadn't been for a long, long time. It was wonderful. It was everything I could ever want our lives together to be. Those few hours were perfect.

When the concert finally ended and we walked back to the underground we were all still singing with the crowd, happy and comfortable in each other's company. Those tickets had given us all a great shift. Togetherness at a time of troubled thinking and separation.

They showed me something important, even though I didn't quite realise it at the time. Just like the song says:

"A simple plot,
That I know one day
Good things are coming our way"

One Door Opens

There is an old saying: - As one door closes another opens

One of my first memories of this saying was my father and Alan Sayers in the Synagogue on Yom Kippur laughing hysterically at the joke: as one door closes another door closes. Well, Yom Kippur is all about closing the door on the old year, making an ending so the New Year can begin with Rosh Hashanah a short time later.

How often have opening doors been significant in my life?

I always saw opening doors as a good thing, something to go through into the place beyond. I didn't stop to look, I saw every one as an opportunity, like there was no decision to make! I romped through them, enthusiastic, full of hope and expectation. They led in lots of different directions – it doesn't feel like I took the direct route. I took one of those shortcuts my dad knew that always took longer, or so my mum said. But then I didn't have a particular destination in mind, so only looking back on it can I see some of the twists and turns. Did it work out well? Who knows? It got me here, didn't it? to the man I am today.

Then there were the closed doors, the ones where I knew, or thought I knew, exactly what was behind them. It was something I really wanted – I was so sure then. I camped out at some of those doors. Hoping and willing them to open, often to no avail. Strange how, just when you lost interest, the door opened anyway. Or when you wandered back past the door sometime later you realised it had been open all the time and you just didn't try the knob. All that energy, worry, time expended!

Do my doors define me? No, I was always me. I don't think I'd do anything different. I still think of the world as charged with good. Maybe I'm not so ambitious as I was? I know something about life, something about me. Maybe I know more about what I want for my life now. Or maybe that all matters less. When I'm good I know it's about letting life flow and seeing what comes, but I still get caught trying to make something happen.

Then I'd see my hands gripping the wheel again and feel the furrows in my brow as I frowned and I'd think to myself, "What am I doing? Lighten up!" I don't think it endeared me to my loved ones either. I think they just saw a black storm cloud circling about my head, like a cartoon character, and steered well clear. Not good!

The great news is that all the doors are different, however much they might look exactly the same. I still open them with the same gusto and excitement. What I don't do is try to force them open like I used to. Waste of time and energy! And when they do open I might see some similarities in the place beyond to situations I had been in before. I might even decide not to go there. Might ...

The even better news is that I back myself. I have skills and experience. I have talent. They arm me and power me, like a character in a role-playing game. I know that with each door that opens, I know more, experience more, am more.

One thing I know clearly is that I still love the adventure of it. Opening doors is worth it. All part of life's great experience. As Eckharte Tolle says: "Life is the dancer and you are the dance".

Why not just let it happen and enjoy it along the way.

Do you choose it?

This life you are living, do you choose it?
Take each day, each thing you do in that day, do you choose it?
Do you choose to follow your passion?
Do you choose your heart's desire?
Your dreams can come true and no, it's not Peter Pan

Who do you share your dreams with?
And do they delight and share them with you?
Whether it's a small thing like walking the dogs
Or something bigger like sailing the oceans blue
Where is your love?
Where is your passion?
Set it free, now, while you have a chance

How brilliant that life would be
Living as one, individuals and together
You can have that ... allow it ... you deserve it
And every day will be the best day
Your future will be bright
You'll want for nothing
And wonder why you didn't do it years ago

How could life be fun every day?

Well, there's a question.

Today I wrote to my family that I had spent a lot of my life looking in the shadows and not enjoying the sunshine. Yesterday I finally realised that my long-held beliefs, the ones I thought defined success for me, were just not real and not true either. They might create money, but they created worries of lack, too. They might create control over life, but they limited just how open I can be to life. Okay, they might just avoid the lows, but to deny myself the blissful highs can't be right, can it? I just get to survive at best. Is that all I want? Doesn't sound like success to me. What do you think?

For me, the above paragraph is BIG! It's my biggest myths exploded. I didn't get that yesterday, but today it's like my glass ceiling, the one that was holding me down from being all I can be, just shattered. That feels really great, like opening a door to a wonderful place that I hadn't seen before. It was always there for me, but I was too busy working and worrying in my own little world to ever see it – until just now.

Today I felt free to cry in the name of love, care and happiness. That might sound silly to you – a grown man crying? I used to think like that, too. Do you know how often I've done that in my life? Probably never! It's a first, a sign that I can really touch life from this place. I can sense life much more clearly. That feels wonderful, like the freshness you smell just after summertime rain. Gentle, soothing and soft. I breathe so much more easily right now. Here comes the sun - the Beatles got it just right.

Today I did my usual work with a different intention. It wasn't a struggle or a grind. I can see it in a new context of building me towards my dreams, my future:

… Walking the dog on the beach every day, hand in hand with my life partner … we spend our days serving our communities locally and round the world … giving freely and receiving with grace and gratitude … living is light and easy … the sun shines … and there is enough … enough without the attachment of too much … oh we have our hard times, when things don't go quite right … sometimes we work long and put ourselves out, but it's all wholesome and worthwhile … and our day ends with a beautiful sunset and a loving kiss …

There, I've said it aloud.

I first saw this dream a year ago, one Sunday in March; a glimpse, then gone in a merry dance. I was still moving to the old tunes and trying out new steps. No wonder it didn't all fit! I believe life gives us lessons, and if we don't learn the lesson, we will continue to bump into more opportunities until we learn. This happened to me a lot, showing me the lessons I needed to learn, even if I didn't see it there and then. It was a crazy time, it took a lot of my energy, but I see how worthwhile it was for me. It got me there – here – to this place of knowing today. Fantastic!

And without a conscious decision, the road opens up in front of me. All I have to do is start walking. It's moving me closer to my dream.

Suddenly all the strands of work that I am doing right now seem to fit together. They line up, like a bunch of stepping-stones across the rushing water to a magic place beyond. There my ultimate work lives, built from all those steps. A wonderful life's work. OMG! The great people we are going to connect with along the way!

These are the reasons to go to bed feeling that today was a great day and waking up with excitement and anticipation for the day to come. I see that now.

Coldplay *Hurts like Heaven* should be playing right now.

And I come back to the present moment and give thanks for having these thoughts in this moment and feeling as good as I feel right now. I choose this life, to be this present from this moment on.

Leap of faith

With a new dream we set off. Full of hope and anticipation. Like magic, our new home appeared, a beautiful place in a small market town, nestled into the north edge of the Yorkshire Moors. Just when no places seemed to be on the market that suited us, one house came available, literally just as we were about to give up the search.

It was a great start to the next part of the journey. It was just perfect, all the way down to the enamelled roll-top bath, the conservatory and the view of the cricket club pitches behind. There's nothing like a cricket match in Yorkshire. Synchronicity in action. We just knew it was the place. No decision to be made. The sun shone in my world.

It was truly wonderful! The purple of the summer heather high on the moors, the amazing views down into the dales. Quaint little York stone villages. With what remained of the summer we discovered the magical coastline of the northeast: Runswick Bay, Staithes, Maske and Saltburn-by-the-sea. I hadn't realised that there was such beauty there.

It's delightful. Go visit if you ever get a chance. Every visit to the moors was a treasure. Each visit to the beach a delight. We walked the dog, flew kites, walked hand in hand by the surf, even in the cold of mid-winter. It was my dream come true. My heaven on Earth!

We discovered a wonderful place, Be All You Can, founded by two fantastic Social Entrepreneurs, Sue Anderson and Bernie

Parks. The impact they've both had in the Teesside area is a fantastic and worthy story. They both deserve a medal! One of our big intentions in moving here was to create community and be of service. We offered our services immediately. It felt like the door was opening to the perfect future.

At the same time I picked up the yoke again and started working on the business. I started a new bank account and paid myself a little more month on month. As things grew, bit by bit, we lived from that small pot of money. It felt good to be starting with a clean slate. I had found a path that seemed easy and light to support both families. Finally. Living simply felt good, too. We had enough for food and a few luxuries, such as organic vegetables, but not much more. There was no need for a lavish lifestyle. We had the forests, the moors and the beach. What more riches did a man need?

Each day I would walk the dog, purposefully and with intent. I'm not sure that I was very present and it was not until much later that I discovered the beauty of the forest in winter. That focus from the walk then powered me on to my computer. Plugging myself into the internet and accelerating up to full speed, I worked through the day and into the evening, on the next deal, the next development, fixing issues, talking to people across continents. I was immersed.

Can you tell that I was controlling life again? What was I doing? Hadn't I learned that lesson yet? Clearly not! B started bringing lunch and dinner to my desk. I got angry with that. I was angry with me. It wasn't a way of life that I wanted. It was a sign, a warning sign, but once again I didn't take note.

My focus became quite myopic. I had a goal to reach. Building something that would provide for everyone. It became my priority and I was getting there, it was going to happen, just a matter of time. Then we'd be ready to move on our dreams, when we had a firm foundation to support us and not before. The love, the sharing, the intimacy came a distant second, again!

Oh dear, the old me had returned and taken hold, pushing the dream aside. Most unlike me for the end to justify the means, but that was what was happening, more and more. I guess I knew I could get results like this, even though it was a struggle and didn't create an ideal life; and wasn't that exactly what I'd gone on my journey for, to find the new me?

Then Christmas came. A time for family and friends. We suddenly noticed that despite good intentions and invites, nobody was joining us for the big day. That didn't feel good. We brushed over it in our way. Worse was that I did my old-style Xmas humbug about the money we were spending on seemingly wasteful presents, and was not good at receiving mine, even though they were given with love. Yes, the old me was definitely back.

I went to London for my daughters 21st celebrations with the other part of my family. Things were strained – not outwardly: in a classic British way. Instead of staying on to really enjoy that moment with my beautiful, talented daughter I felt strained and couldn't really enjoy myself. To top it all, I had leave early to catch a train. Not satisfactory. Now it seemed I couldn't be comfortable wherever I was. I was way off track and still heading in the wrong direction. Why wasn't I listening to my compass?

The only event that was a real celebration was the Xmas Party at Be All You Can. Here was a real sense of Community and real Xmas spirit. Yet we hadn't really found the right way to engage with them and help grow and nurture that community. I was nonplussed. A big warning was sounding in my heart by now.

Was I being impatient? Suddenly it seemed the dream I'd dreamt was not what I was creating. My head and the plan were ruling. Why had I abandoned the new life that I'd discovered, living and sharing day by day?

I tried harder, hoping for a better tomorrow, one that was just round the corner, I was sure of it. I pushed, prodded and cajoled, mostly myself, but the people around me, too. They weren't helping me. They were getting in the way of the Great Plan. I was starting to sound like Charlie Chaplin's Great Dictator. Someone find me a giant inflatable globe that I can kick around the room, quick!

This was how my behaviour had changed. I'd forgotten the new me. I'd lost sight of my beautiful dream. Love was off the agenda, in the name of progress and stability. I think I felt once again that I was the only one who was going to climb the mountain and I was going to carry them all up to the summit. Come hell or high water. Is this a good way to be in the world?

I'd already figured that it didn't serve me before, so why was I doing it again? I guess it was just a simple misunderstanding. What is it they say about believing your own bullshit? You must be reading this and saying to yourself, "Why doesn't this guy learn his lessons?" I can't tell you, except to say that I thought I was doing the right thing for us all.

This went on for some months. Far too long. Don't get me wrong, action is good. Direction, purpose and progress, all good. From a business perspective it did bear fruit. Things were really starting to get going. Maybe it's why I did things in that way, because I knew it would get a result. But where was the heart? Where was the love for me and everyone around me?

I had postponed it for the day when I could have enough. What was enough? I could have had that love in my life every day. With my partner, my family, my friends; but I denied myself. Those little touches, those fantastic intimacies between a man and a woman all dried up in the name of getting there. What a shame! When you stop and think about it, how important are they in your life? Call me Ebenezer Scrooge, why don't you?

It was my "Trouble in Paradise".

At the double!

Tension had been building for a while now – tension in me, tension due to being progressively estranged from my children and family; tension with B, between my efforts to provide and our joint efforts to create the life we wanted, and as a result of my efforts to stay connected with my other family. Most worrying of all, the love, intimacy and sharing that had made our life together so special seemed to have withered in the face of all this thinking.

For a long time I had been noticing the people around me. The ones who particularly came to my attention were the ones who were stuck. I can always see the massive potential in people. One of my superpowers maybe, or are we all like that when we meet the world in a generous mood? They, on the other hand, were either totally missing it, or they were resisting like mad the thing they were born to do. I guess my own personal approach is to be in motion, moving somewhere, growing, developing. It's just what feels natural to me.

So why weren't these folk on their hero's journey? Oh, they are ready to go, or they might even be part way, but at that point they are stuck, dithering. Does that sound unkind? I guess it might, but I so want them to do well. I want everyone to do well. That's just me I guess. I'd give money, no, I *have* given money, time and effort to help them do well. I don't seem to be that successful at it. I often wondered why that was.

Then I happened to listen to the great Jim Rohn again one day in the car on the long route to home. He said something about, "How you are showing up in the world is who you are attracting".

... BOOM!

I got it, right between the eyes. All these stuck people were showing me that I was stuck too! That was so valuable for me, a man who likes to be in motion. I had also been noticing people who were taking action. I so wanted to be like them. I thought I was taking steps. I so wanted to be moving forward and suddenly I knew how this was creating a tension inside of me. My alarm bells were working overtime and now I knew why. It was time to get moving.

There was a big downside to this, though. B, the woman I loved – love – appeared to me to be stuck, too. Well, I attracted her didn't I? I had been encouraging and supporting her to get moving, but each time I did anything in this area she saw it as criticism and pressure. So instead of helping, much as I really wanted her to be the massive success I saw possible for her, I was becoming the problem. There was a tension building there, too. A tension that love couldn't overcome – or that was the way it seemed.

Finally, I went to an event where the people there were on the move, full of possibility and creating their future. It felt like home, like success. I knew what needed to happen. I came home – well, back to the place we lived anyway. On the way I tried to communicate with B about getting moving, but all it did was increase the tension.

My impression of B, on the other hand, was that she had another story, another issue in mind, one that hadn't occurred to me and was very different to mine. I thought I heard her say that she wanted me to declare for her completely: divorce, marriage and so on. It hadn't been an issue before, but it seemed to have become a big thing for her – and I didn't even see that. How could I NOT have seen that? I was so committed to making things work, for us, for her, and it was all coming right – wasn't it? As I write this I still don't know exactly what was going on for her, but the tension between us was palpable. It was like the San Andreas Fault line ready for the earthquake, with us on either side. It was the brink of disaster, disaster that felt very real for both of us.

That two people in what had been in such a magical relationship had created this was unthinkable. We had arrived in two very different places, with very strong needs for ourselves, so strong they transcended all the love and feeling we held for each other.

We were both off track at this point. Now I look back I see this as the ultimate test on my hero's journey, and it came with a BIG price!

I'm sure B would recount this story differently to the way I've set it out. Her story is true, too, and very real for her – I totally accept that. Amazing how, as human beings, we all interpret situations differently and create our experience of life from that interpretation. Neither of us were wrong or right, but our thoughts were very different and they meant that we saw ourselves, our needs and our relationship very differently - San Andreas for sure!

It was just too much ...

... and after a long struggle ...

... we came to the end.

In a highly charged couple of days we undid the work of almost two years together. One night she opened her arms to welcome me home from the snow and I just sat there, numb, on the sofa, while she tried to hold my hand and just be with me. I was in meltdown. That's the result of all the controlling I was doing.

After that we didn't speak, we hardly touched. Something was so badly wrong. Any communication we had seemed to be a monologue. Connection severed. Number unobtainable. I still can't believe it to this day. It was ludicrous, stupid even. How had it come to this? I still don't know and it hurts just to think about it..

She got to go her way and I could take my next step, too. It felt so wrong. And yet, all at the same time, it also felt right. I console myself with the thought that this was the perfect next step for both of us. Okay, there were short-term issues, like where to live and so on, but suddenly I felt like I had the freedom to move, the space to breathe again. I'd been trying so hard and now that the reason for that had gone it was such a release.

I was mighty sad, too. Love is something not to be given up lightly. A loving relationship is a great gift. It's one of the biggest losses I've ever faced in life. How could we have let it get here? How could we?

B was very brave; she met me at the Lion Pub on Blakey Ridge, high on the moors. I talked. She cried. I held her as she tried to be strong. It was relief for a moment, but it didn't really change anything, much as either of us might have wanted it to.

It hurt badly. Think about losing something that you hold really dear to you. Something that means a lot, and I mean A LOT. Contemplate losing that, and you might get close to feeling what I was feeling.

Maybe the most love you can ever experience is letting go and letting your loved one free to fly. I found that love. I experienced life in a new and more meaningful way. It was so hard, but a massive lesson that I know will serve me well for the rest of my life.

Fly well B x

Over the next few weeks I got angry and smashed plates, cried, laughed at the relief of the clarity I had now that deep-held tension was gone, and tried to look back and celebrate the love that we both had for each other, even though the relationship was gone.

My main companion in those weeks was our chocolate Lab. Aren't dogs great? They are your friends without any conditions. He never judged me once and he was always there for me. I took him for walks up to Highcliffe Peak – he loved the walk, loved nature and being out. I tried to follow his lead, but there was just too much going on in my head. I couldn't bear the beauty and the silence. Stan was patient with me all this time. He was such a friend.

It was a time of scudding black clouds, heavy rain and occasional glimpses of sun. Both B and I mourned the beauty of what had been whilst stepping forward on our respective new paths. I was surprised that life hadn't stopped in its tracks, but everything moves on, each day taking us further apart. It was made all the harder by the need to dismantle what should have been our happy home, nestled in the beauty of the moors.

We worked together, in a polite and restrained way that was so unlike us. That magnified my whole experience, because it showed us exactly how our relationship had changed, and just what we'd lost. I hated the idea of leaving the moors, too. This loss was something I was really struggling to come to terms with.

On the one hand I felt like I had been just getting started in our new life and things were just about to be everything we'd hoped they would be. On the other, the tensions between our very different needs meant that we were both struggling to live our "best lives", the ones that had felt so important to us at the outset of our beautiful journey. Our beautiful years, as B had once called them. It was unbelievable that it had come to this. Like living in a waking dream.

Even after the break-up I loved her, still love her, although we are not going to be together any more. I was highly frustrated. It was like a mathematical equation that couldn't be solved. I kept wondering if I'd got my methods and reasoning wrong, and if I just got that right then everything would work out. But no, it wasn't to be. Sometimes it's just not meant to be, I suppose, but deep down I couldn't accept that.

I'd thought B was my Mavis from *Synchronicity*. Mavis was a lifetime partner, whether she was together with her man or not. They spent three years on different continents, but still very much a couple. It turned out not to be the case for us. From the outset B always said that we were meant to be together for the rest of our lives.

Who were we to think we would follow someone else's journey, even Joe Jaworski's? Everyone has their own journey and this turned out to be ours. Well, our time together will serve in our futures, lovely memories, a time of growth and important lessons in life. For both of us. In that way I know we will always be together. Maybe that will be consolation someday. Until then I'll honour her anyway.

Life has its seasons. It's inevitable. And just like the end of winter on the Yorkshire Moors where I was living, where the bulbs were starting to sprout, spring was coming for me, too. I could feel it, the warm sunshine and good times were coming around again. The opportunity to live my "best life" again. I got to go my way without the tensions and stresses that had been quietly building over recent months. That felt good.

Everything was suddenly much clearer. Amazing how we forget and let ourselves wander off our perfect path without even knowing it. Even better, we have the ability to realise that we are off course and get back on it. This was a major course correction, but a necessary one for both of us.

You know, there's a lot of talk about legacies. I used to worry about that. What was I leaving as my legacy in life? Apart from two great kids, of course. Give me a slap will you? Two great kids is enough! But indulge me a moment ...

I like the view of 9th Wonder (a US rap artist) when he says, "You don't decide your legacy, others decide it for you." There is also a piece in the Jewish Scripture, The Talmud, that says:

"Whosoever preserves a single soul, scripture ascribes [merit] to him as though he had preserved a complete world."

For me this means that if you help one person, you help the world. I think my legacy will be the opportunities I created or facilitated or supported for a whole bunch of people. Whether all those people took those opportunities, or even if they got what I had hoped for, I'm glad to have been part of their growth. I think of myself as generous. Well, generosity, in my book, is giving without expecting anything in return. I did that, most of the time. It has always served me and felt right to live this way. Think about the legacies you've already left. You may not have solid bricks and mortar, things like buildings or scholarships, but I'll bet you've created loads of opportunity, too. You've fully played your part in the dance.

The opportunity that this relationship had given both of us was huge and I took some comfort from that in those early days of the break-up. I know that I will always meet life this way, looking to create wonderful opportunities. As a good friend told me then, "When you start something that feels very right and wholesome you never know how its going to turn out". I'll take that chance, again and again. Now that's what I call Life!

Nothing to do

I always wanted a pair of gloves like the cowboys wore. Think of John Wayne sitting on a fidgeting pony and delivering one of his quintessential glib one-liners. Then focus in on his hands, holding the reins, effortlessly controlling the nervy mount underneath him. Those gloves.

I used to go to America a fair bit, in my corporate days and to visit my dad. I often spent time looking for gloves, those gloves, gloves a cowboy might wear. Short, tan leather gloves. My search was persistent and long. I had to buy these perfect gloves, but I couldn't seem to find them. Eventually I stopped looking. Then one day I went down to a local animal feed store near where my father lives in New Hampshire. I was bound to find a pair of proper cowboy gloves in a place like this, I thought.

It was an old, red, wooden-clad building with an inbuilt dock for loading wagons. Family run, it specialised in everything for animals, but mostly horses. I bought two pairs of gloves there: one black pair, thermal and thin, that I still use with my best coat even though the seams are starting to part. They only cost 60c – great gloves, and what a bargain! Sometimes great things appear when you least expect, don't they?

The other pair were meant to be my cowboy gloves. They had a choice in the store. They were tan leather, too, but none of them reminded me of JW's gloves. They were too thick and loose fitting surely? They were the wrong colour, too, a solid tan brown. Why couldn't I find a pair of proper JW cowboy gloves? Even in a place like this? I bought a pair anyway. Hell, it wasn't that much money and gloves always come in handy in the English winter.

And that was the end of my search for cowboy gloves. I put that thought aside and the dream seemed to fade. I just carried on with my life, with other things on my mind. As people do. Maybe it just wasn't meant to happen? After all, can anybody else own John Wayne's gloves?

Looking back at it now, I see that my search for my "best life" had been a lot like that. Looking, seemingly in vain, for something that seemed to elude me. Oh, I'd found my dream of the perfect life, "walking hand in hand, a loving kiss at the end of the day." I'd had it and let it slip away – again. In fact, the harder I searched and tried, the less I seemed to find that life. I got more focused and every day the search intensified. I was very persistent, too. Like the JW gloves, I had this idea that I would find or create the perfect situation for me, for us, that it was out there somewhere, but, just like John Wayne's perfect riding gloves, my perfect life hadn't appeared – yet!

Then one day I noticed something. I was on the platform, waiting for the London train. It was a bit cold. You know that old damp cold that we get in England in the winter. I dug in the pocket of my jacket and came out with a pair of gloves. Those tan leather gloves, the ones I bought in New Hampshire all those years ago. You don't know how good that made me feel. It was like magic.

I put them on without a thought and it was then that I realised I'd had my JW gloves all along! They are old now, wrinkled and worn. The dye has run and faded. Suddenly they fit me perfectly and they look just great. Just like John Wayne. Where's my pony? I'll put my pistol in one hand and my rifle in the other and face the world from my strongest place. True grit!

During the tumultuous break-up with B I had an experience that was very much like this. Just as she and I were battling with ideas about taking action in life, divorce and marriage, and the split became inevitable, something else appeared for me. A very important and special something. My family.

I suddenly had a huge insight. During all the time that I had been off searching for my "best life", I had been carrying a building tension that was missing being with my family. I went back to see them all regularly, but we all struggled with it in our minds. My brother later said of that time that he felt I had left and wondered whether I would ever come back. I love my family. All of them. Don't you?

No matter how your relationship is right now with your family members, your kids are always your kids and your parents are always your parents. They are the ones you love, conditionally and unconditionally, you just can't help it. I realised now that being without them had cost me a lot more than I'd ever thought; now I had the opportunity to set that right.

Suddenly, just like running with the bulls, there was no decision to make, I just knew: I knew that all roads led back home. That uncomfortable tension I'd had with Lucy for the last two years could come to an end now and we could find a new way to be together. Like we had when we were younger and full of love. I knew how to be that man now. I'd missed them all so much, without even realising it. It was the one thing I could do now, to rebuild those important connections and get that part of my life right. Even if there was ever an outside chance of continuing a relationship with B, I knew it would need to include my family. So any which way I looked at it, going home made sense. A lot of sense.

It was like I'd suddenly found my John Wayne gloves. They were the perfect fit, the perfect look. Just perfect. They'd been waiting for me all along. When I'd been searching so hard for my "best life", it was waiting for me all that time. Why had my wife, Lucy, not pressed for divorce as she had been advised by others around her? I guess she knew something I didn't. Clever girl!

There was no decision to make. It was totally obvious what the next steps were and over the next few weeks I reconnected with my father, brother, wife and kids. It was all so good. I was finally able to share my journey with them again. Tension eased. Forgiveness and reconciliation were never in doubt. If you are loved − I mean truly loved − you'll always be forgiven, I guess, but it felt great all the same.

Lucy was the key. I met her in a hotel to see if the connection we had once had was still there. It's amazing how you can rekindle a flame, even if the fire has sunk to ash and embers. I could still feel the warmth and so could she. It was like a brand new start for us. Yes, we had that companionship and connection that we'd always had, but now there was more for us. That felt exciting. Really exciting. It felt real.

It was a lovely warm feeling to start to get them all back in my life. So welcome. Now I really could ride just like John Wayne in the movies. I was strong, powerful and confident, too. I would go back to my family armed with all the lessons I had learned in these two years and much more able to live my "best life" with them all. Remember *Hurts like Heaven*? Well, this was my time.

In fact, the song that was playing inside me then was *Let Your Soul be Your Pilot* by Sting. Again, the music was telling me something. This was a song that Lucy and I had shared a long time before and it seemed even more relevant now, for both of us.

How did it happen? It seemed that just when I wasn't looking, not chasing, not frustrated and desperate for something to happen, that's the moment it did. In this case I was caught up in a very different situation when this massive opportunity popped up in front of me.

Or was it that my thinking changed and I just saw my life differently, just like I saw the gloves differently?

What made my gloves as special as John Wayne's, a movie hero? Just living everyday life. You know – walking the dog, commuting, generally keeping my hands warm, nothing special. Yet they had accompanied me and become a part of my life, familiar. It just goes to prove that, even when it seems like I am doing nothing, things are happening for me and I'm becoming the superhero. Just being with my family, and then not being with them, but caring about them all the same, had made them a perfect fit. I guess they always were, but it took me this whole journey to see that. "Silly man", I hear you say. I laugh out loud because you are so right! At the same time, I could have missed this "jewel in my crown" easily for a long time. I'm very glad now that I found it.

When I set my unconscious mind, my intention, to something, it never gives up. My intention was always that my family was one of the biggest things in my life. It found the way. If I had thought how that would happen, should happen, it never would. In two years of trying to create new relationships with my family it hadn't happened, until this moment.

Maybe there's a market for worn retro John Wayne gloves? After all, everyone wants to be a superhero; but then, aren't we already there and just pretending that we aren't ? Aren't we all the real-life Incredibles?

The Little Naseberry Tree

In 2010, almost before this big chapter in my life had opened, I went to Jamaica on holiday at a wonderful cliffside hotel in Negril. It was meant to be a birthday celebration. Paradise, you might think. Actually it was far from a happy week. My mum was in the late stages of terminal illness and my thoughts about her and about what was about to happen weighed heavily on me. I couldn't enjoy myself, despite the sunshine, the facilities and the cool people. I had brief interludes where the sun shone in my head, but mostly it was dark, very dark. What a waste, I know.

On the night of my birthday dinner we went to a small cove where the waves crashed dramatically against the rocks. It was most unusual for the Caribbean Sea to be so rough, and in that crashing ferment I realised that the job I was doing, the business I was running, was all wrong; not only was I going to lose my mum, but I also had to set a new direction in my life. The waves were crashing in my head, too.

As I think about it now, this was right at the start of my journey, the one I've set out in these pages, anyway. I didn't realise it then, but this was a big moment in my life.

Amidst all the tumult of that week there was a moment one morning where I found something that turned out to have very special meaning for me and for my immediate family, too. A small seemingly insignificant thing as you'll see ...

Every morning I'd come down to breakfast and have the fruit plate, because it was full of wonderful fresh fruit and very healthy for me, so I thought. Some of the fruit I'd never come across before. Ever tasted a Naseberry? No? Its like a cross between looking and tasting like a plum, but with the texture of a pear. Very tasty.

The plate would come beautifully prepared, with all the fruit cut and ready to eat. One morning my Naseberry slice had a stone in it. Rather than discarding it, something in me told me to keep the stone and have a go at growing it at home. Now, I'm a man with very little interest in gardening, so this was most unlike me, but I did it anyway. It just felt like the thing to do. That breakfast fruit was one of the small breaks in the clouds of my mind that week and would shine a bright ray of light into my life later on.

I got home, found a pot and some earth, planted the Naseberry stone and left it somewhere warm and sunny. I wondered if it would grow. Nothing happened for some while and then, quite magically, something began to sprout from the soil in the pot. A single shoot that, steadily, day on day, week on week, month on month, turned into a twig. It was magical! Then it grew a couple of leaves. It just kept growing, very slowly, almost imperceptibly, more height, more leaves and then a side branch. I was witnessing one of life's miracles.

And all it needed was a bit of water from time to time and a sunny spot. Nothing much. The Naseberry knew what to do. It didn't need to discover itself or figure out the meaning of life.

It is Life.

And all through my journey the little Naseberry tree has been doing this. Patient, steady growth, like it knows exactly what it's meant to be and it's just doing it. At the same time I was off searching, working, figuring life out and me with it. Loving and losing and loving again. Fortunately Lucy felt the Naseberry like I did – she kept it watered and even re-potted it. Even though I'd completely moved out of the house, and only came back infrequently, both Lucy and I cared for the Naseberry. It was telling us something about us, about life, patience and caring. It was telling us something about love.

During the two years of this journey I learned so much about love. More than in the last thirty years. I'm really grateful for that – it's HUGE. Hard to explain, but let me try.

Giving love is the greatest thing you can ever do. That little Naseberry just loves life, it is life. It knows what to do. It just shows up in the world. It doesn't have to be anything other than the beautiful little tree that it is becoming. At that level everything is just so simple. It had a message for me, for us. One that, without listening very hard, we were both hearing. Just keep on loving, whatever is happening in your life. Even when we weren't together, we were still in love and just like the Naseberry we didn't need to know it.

We just were. I guess that's why divorce never entered our minds. We'd been connected for such a long time and that was fundamental to both of us. At its simplest, when we had nothing else we both loved that little Naseberry and it loved us and everything around it. It was just being. It had nowhere to go, nothing it had to do. Growing was completely natural for it. It just is.

That little Naseberry showed me that Love is the greatest gift to you and to everyone you give your love to. Like the tree, you have boundless amounts of love in you, so why not? Everyone and every living thing has that superpower in them, waiting to come out. Doesn't it feel good to love and care for someone and something?

It might be painful sometimes, but it also deeply satisfies your soul, and to me that's the richest experience you can ever have.

Let's turn back the pages here, to the start of the story. I mentioned wealth, didn't I? And I'll bet you thought wealth was money. I certainly did, but then I figured out that time is really important. Not just the sixteenth piece in the puzzle, but quality time to really enjoy and be grateful for everything you've got. Time became more important for me than money. At the end of this journey it's clear to me that love transcends both time and money.

Love is real wealth ...

... it's the only currency.

So love is really all there is! When you see that, nothing else matters. I've seen love through different eyes and in lots of different ways now. Now I know how my dream can be made real. It's not a place to get to or something that has to be achieved. It's in us every day, ready to burst forth with its gifts. We just seem to forget sometimes. I forgot, and paid a heavy price, but now I remember more and more.

It doesn't matter about the clouds, when they appear and whatever they are created from – the past, the future, habitual thinking – they all pale into insignificance when you just love. For love's sake alone. It's a most wonderful way to be in the world.

So now I put love first and last. At the start of the day I love my partner, my kids and everyone around, cherish them and want everything good for them. At the end of the day I'm so grateful for what I've got and what they've given me. Regardless of everything that's in the bulk of the day – the work, the problems, the interruptions, the details – this is what's important. I don't need to be anywhere special. On the beach or not, hand in hand or separated by thousands of miles. I'm still in love – with life.

That was what that little stone from a breakfast plate was here to show me. It gave me a bright ray of sunshine that breaks through the worst clouds, sooner or later. I'll end my journey here for the moment, knowing that I'll forget at some point, get lost, go on my hero's journey once more, maybe; but I know that I'll remember again because somewhere deep down inside me is my stone that I can plant again, and it will sprout and grow again. Love is always there for me and I'm so happy for that.

PART THREE

THE PAY-OFF

"We shall not cease from exploration
And the end of all our exploring
Will be to arrive where we started
And know the place for the first time"

T S Eliot

It's Only Me

So what was this journey to find me? This big change to my life? Why did I change so much of my circumstances, try so many different things, search so hard to find me? How could I be lost?

You know what? I was always there, I was always me. How could I not be?

Like I said right at the start of the journey, it was just about remembering. You see, I'd just plain forgotten who I was, who I am. All I needed to do was remember. Why was that so hard? One reason: habitual thinking.

By habitual thinking I mean that over the course of my life I'd picked up notions and ideas, some of them handed down from my parents, by just watching the way they lived and from my strong desire to be a son to be proud of. Other things included wanting to be a good husband and father myself. Nothing wrong with that, it's true. Then there is a notion that a lot of guys like me have, to be the hunter-gatherer, bringing food to the table and being "the leader".

I was another kind of leader, too. In corporate life I rose to a point where hundreds of people reported to me and I toured the country, the western world, in the name of customers and big business. That was important for me, but I see now that it was just a story, one that I don't need to follow. I paid a high price for that lesson, but I know it's worth it for the freedom that I feel more and more in my life today.

Some of my habitual thinking I used like protective armour. Certain situations I would avoid. People have always said that I'm a bit brusque and cold on first meeting. Of course it's not true; I am a warm and welcoming guy, always willing to extend the hand of friendship to someone new, to find their goodness and help them on their way. How could these two views be so different? Which was right?

I think they both were – are – but my habitual thinking held me back meeting new people and when people didn't respond to me I hid comfortably behind the thought of, "Oh well, they are just seeing me as the brusque guy". It probably also made me avoid opportunities where I would be seen in that way. I went out less. What opportunities did I miss because of that? Maybe that kind of thing happens to you?

Never mind. I'm over it now, most of the time.

Beyond that, I was one of Maggie Thatcher's children. I grew up in an era when materialism was good. Our idea of visiting somewhere new was to go shopping and buy the unique stuff that came from that part of the world. This was a big one for me: what car I drove, the house I lived in, affording everything so our kids wanted for nothing. That started with brand new prams, through to riding lessons and then horses. The financial burdens got bigger and bigger, managing loans and credit became the norm, looking for the next 0% balance transfer offer and trying to figure out how to get a pension plan that would actually be worth something. In my backgammon game the bet doubled regularly and often. I was that Boiling Frog I mentioned right at the start of this story.

Looking back on it that's a lot of baggage. It created a lot of thought, too. Maybe you can see where my Monday morning thinking came from. Yes, it created lots of thinking, worrying, figuring and scheming. I always admired the Zen Buddhist idea that each situation should be dealt with properly and fully. When done, even if it was not finished, it should be put away and not noticed until the next time. I tried to do that – but in my book, trying and doing are completely different things.

Most often I had a stream of things going through my mind, like juggling lots of balls or solving the sixteen-piece puzzle I mentioned earlier. Add the last piece and you jam up the works – simple as that. Is that why men are meant to be so bad at multitasking? Actually I'm not sure that women are much better, but boy do they get to do more, as mum, professional, wife, friend and lover; what choice do they have? But you've always got a choice, to remember who you really are and what is real for you.

That's how I forgot me, how I got lost. I was distracted, busy, too. I put skeletons in the cupboard and hoped nobody would find them; above all, so that I could ignore them for a little while. The price I paid was that I lived a life that was only a vague facsimile of the life I would have chosen to live. There's an old Confucian saying, it's a curse actually – most people don't know it or misquote it:

"*May you live in interesting times ... and not know it.*"

Well I was missing out!

All I had to do was drop the baggage and let go of all that thinking and I was still right there, where I had always been. All I had to do! As you've read, some old beliefs are not so easy to let go of – well for me, anyway. When I was weighed down I had so little room to breathe, so little time to listen to my wisdom. So little time to love – that was the big one!

It's like swimming. You don't need to learn how to float. You did that in the first nine months, didn't you? No effort required, no learning, no trying. It's built in, a fully-functioning feature of our makeup. I remember my son, Ben: as soon as he could totter to the edge of a pool he'd jump right in. Parents used to gasp and be afraid for him, but he was just fine. My daughter, Helen, would climb very carefully into the pool and hold on to the side. Hard! A very different approach. Somehow she'd already forgotten that if you just lie back and relax, you float. It's a skill we all have. Eventually she did remember – we always do. Well, I'd forgotten, too.

Maybe what happens is that as you float you pick up something, thinking it will help you float, then something else and another item. At first it may well help, but sooner or later you find it dragging you under. Not good! Time to let that stuff go, relax, and get floating again.

At one point I didn't even realise that I was NOT choosing how to live. I was carrying so much stuff and working so hard just to stay above water. That was where all the control and grasping at life came from. I had to stay afloat. I just had to! I felt like my life depended on it. It was only when I started a coaching programme with the fantastic Jamie Smart that I realised my innate abilities – like floating and my inner compass – were hidden away deep in my memory, exactly because I was kicking so hard against my natural flow. I was pointed in a different direction to where I should be headed, trying to get "there". So the journey I undertook, my hero's journey, was my commitment to choose to live as I would really want to.

For me, that turned into the two-year trip that I've described to you in these pages, at the end of which I know it's not the end. Of course.

A big part of the journey was that along my road I had what I called landslides. I think it was the coaching events – after each one I'd feel tired and down, like some pain or memory was leaving my body and mind. Could I tell you exactly what that was? No, but after that everything felt so much better. I was more grounded. Some of that baggage had left me. I was more able to be me. Able to listen to my own intuition.

B, my partner on this journey, did in three weeks the letting go that took me six months. What an avalanche that must have been! But maybe that's an easier road in the end because my two years were littered with resisting letting go, trying hard to fix things and frustration that I wasn't there. As you'll have read, my journey to understanding was a rollercoaster ride.

But life has its seasons; to get to appreciate spring and summer there has to be a winter. Work with them all, that's my recommendation. As I've got better and more consistent at showing up as me, the lows have got less and the highs more than I ever had before. It's a fulfilling life and I love it!

I'll bet there's a way to clear out all this thinking without facing the trials, or the expense that I set myself. Everyone does it differently and my path won't be yours, but maybe you've seen some similarities already.

Is it a one-time fix?

Yes and no. You are always there, always free to choose your path, it's just that sometimes you forget or get a little distracted. Eventually you'll realise, let go of whatever it is that is leading you astray and float free once more. I think that's because you just realise quicker that it's your habitual thinking again. Or as Richard Wilkins and Liz Ivory would say, its the Script you are carrying. It's not you!

Like a sailboat, you are built to be self-righting, you'll come back to the right way up. Just give it a bit of time. That's all it needs.

Going right back to Dr Joseph Campbell and his hero's journey, I've been through some challenges: moving home twice and living totally differently, for a start. I've seen my emotional baggage and let it go and sometimes picked it up again without even realising. I had my landslides, too, getting rid of stuff I didn't even consciously know I had. I said goodbye to a lot of materialism – not all though – along the way. I've been ducked and thoroughly wet from life's experience; I've come back for more. Now I'm lighter, clearer, ready to tread the path of discovery and see what's out there for me. I'm ready to love again and be loved. I stand tall and comfortable in my skin – today anyway – and step out with anticipation.

As the great Dr Keith Blevens would say: "You are who you were meant to be."

Doesn't if feel good to hear that? Doesn't that take the pressure off? For me it meant that I could stop trying to be different, stop searching for something that I should be and just be me. I liken it to being a tuning fork. It can only play one note, pure and clear. And all that's required to play is to just be open to love, first and foremost. Then it's all so simple. And no, it's not a trick. In fact it's the greatest gift, you'll see.

Eightsome Reel

Join me in A Scottish Country Dance? It'll be fun!

Slight trepidation of not knowing the dance or the dancers
All strangers together with a purpose
We learn the dance with a short practice verse
And then we're off ...

The familiarity grows as you hear the pattern of verse and
chorus
You start to enjoy and anticipate the bits you know
With each step, almost, you change partners
Who are you going to meet?
So it's something new, too
It's full of action
Engaging all your senses
Grinning now, you abandon yourself to the dance

Who cares about where it goes or how you look
If you make a mistake, everyone is there to guide you
And you guide and encourage them right back
Clapping and stamping your feet right now

You finish, laughing and smiling.
You don't judge yourself ... you just know it was fun!
You totter off the floor for a well-earned rest
Enthused at the experience you step up for more

How much is life like that? How much could life be life that?

If you find yourself in stillness, you will also be present and alive when you are out there in the world in action, too.

It's in the stillness that you find you.

While you are dancing you are engaged, energised and enjoying the ride, I hope. The interesting thing to notice is what happens when you stop. That's when things start to appear and life gets even more interesting.

You could decide to stay on for another dance. No doubt you'll learn new steps, find new partners or meet new people. You could come off the floor for a rest. I'll bet your mind is already starting to mull over the possibilities and make new suggestions for you. How you'd like to do more dancing, get lessons, maybe, or find another venue. You might think no more of it, leave the dance and then a few days later something comes of it. Someone you met there crosses your path again in business or they become a friend in some other way.

Life's Magic Tapestry

How many people are you connected to? Your family, friends, acquaintances and colleagues. Isn't it great to have all those connections? They are one of the things that make life truly interesting. Some of your connections nourish and support you. Others advise, guide. Yet more excite and inspire. You have all kinds of people connecting to you in different ways, creating your life experience. It's not called life's rich tapestry for nothing.

Maybe you have people you don't like, for a variety of reasons, connected with you, too? You are just as connected to them as you are to your friends. What's that old saying about "keep your friends close and your enemies even closer" – see what I mean?

If you wrote down all the people you connect with or have ever connected with in your life, I bet that would fill an address book.

"So I know a lot of people," I hear you say, "so what?"

I'm asking you to think how you are connected with those people. Every meeting, every conversation, every life event you've had is a stitch, a weave in a big tapestry that is your life. It's one that's been weaving all your life, just as everyone that is connected to you has theirs and theirs are connected to yours in one or even many places.

Do you get a sense of that? How big and wonderful these tapestries are and how intricate? What an amazing skill we all have – and it comes quite naturally. In fact try and stop it. You can't!

Have you ever seen a traditional weaver's loom, with threads stretched on the loom and a shuttle to weave threads across and through? There's skill in the weaving. The starting of threads, the changing of a thread and the finishing off of the edges. The rhythm and flow of the shuttle, too. We've been part of a weave all our lives without even knowing it. You may not have realised just how beautiful you are.

Some of your threads are loose ends, unfinished, maybe waiting to be added to or finished off. Who knows what could happen? That's where the real creation is, and why weavers are such skilled artists and craftsmen all in one go. Yet at the same time it's so simple, moving the shuttle through the loom, tying on a new thread and so on. The simple things are often the best, don't you think?

Simple, yet complicated. In my recent past I had lost some long time connections. My mother, for example, was so involved with my weave. She was in every movement of the shuttle, for all my life until she died. Then her thread ended on the tapestry. It fundamentally changed the pattern and my brother's, and also his threads with mine; and then my father's thread with both of us, and my wife and kids. See how one simple change can make a huge difference? For me it wasn't in the change of the weave, but in the contrast between the tapestry in the first part of my life and how it seems now. The colours have changed.

I don't seem to control the weaving in my life. I like some of the changes, but there are so many that all I can do is sit back and watch as I move the shuttle of my life and the threads change, combine and finish, almost without any help from me. Oh, I'd like to control it more, but it's just the way it comes out for me. I try to be satisfied with that. Some parts of my tapestry are fantastic and I wonder at how they were ever created. Other parts don't really work so well, but they are all part of my weave.

It came to me last week that another person I've known for a long time has been busy in his weave, trying to create a particular pattern with great concentration. His whole adult life. He's grabbed the shuttle, changing the threads at his command. He's following a pattern that he particularly wanted to create. That's how it seems to me. He's been pretty successful. Captain of industry, great home and holiday home, too, wife and two kids, expensive cars, travelled the world and so on.

It's exactly what he wanted – only his kids aren't easy at all and his wife is divorcing him. Maybe control doesn't pay? For me it means more effort and emotion. Does it really get the outcome you so desire? Maybe once he's let them take control of their threads and weave for themselves, then a new part of the tapestry will shape and form? Everything as it should be ...

Have you got some tangles in the weave? Pieces that didn't come out straight or colours that clash and you've spent hours looking at them, trying to pick and pry, to make them right, and it's just not happening? The tapestry and the weaving seems a physical thing, something you can see, feel and touch.

I mostly imagine mine as hanging on a wall somewhere quiet, where I can enjoy its intricacy and it can be displayed like the great work of art that it is.

But here's the thing – it has no form, no substance. None at all! The threads are not made of anything physical. The tapestry is actually more like a spiders web: one brush of the hand and you can wipe it away. We all get caught up believing it really exists, when all the time it's just a collection of ideas, thoughts and memories that add colour to the way you see yourself and your life.

It's the way other people see you, too. So why not take this opportunity to see your life differently? With one stroke you can change your life history, see the world afresh, repair all the tangles or see the beauty in them. For me, coming back to my family showed me the old tapestry in a beautiful new way. What could be more beautiful than that?

In truth, even when I was unhappy with the tapestry I was being weaved into at the time, as I gaze back now it all looks pretty amazing to me. Are you getting a sense of the miracle you are part of yet? The best music, an amazing symphony in which you are playing a single part.

Your Feelings Barometer

Do you remember playing a game as a child where someone, usually your parents, hid something in the room and you had to find it. You'd move around the room and your mum would call out "hotter" or "colder" as you got closer or farther away from the hidden item. And when you were very close she'd shout, "You're boiling!" and with glee you'd find the prize. Remember that great game? The feelings barometer is like that.

Today I started the day with the most wonderful present: I had a lie in. I just lay there, with someone very close and special in my arms, warm under the covers. I read a bit of a good book and then lay back and basked in the warmth, knowing that life was perfect, right there, right then. Do you know that kind of feeling? Well, that feeling is telling me that everything is good and I am living the life most natural for me. I'm going with the flow, so to speak, although it's much more about who I am being in this moment, than anything I am doing.

Then I turned on my phone, to find a song stored on it, and a text message came through. In a moment – and I mean a second, no more – I was transformed. I didn't feel good, frustration filled my chest and the day suddenly felt very different. Now, all that happened was a technical issue, and you know yourself that in today's world, systems have issues. It's inevitable.

So, I could get really upset, go into a storming rage and spoil my day. Before, when that happened to me, in my mind I'd start to think of other things to get frustrated about, however petty, like the lawn not being cut or someone who hadn't replied to an email. Can you see how I'm getting strident now even as I write this? It's easy to get off track and end up in a whole heap of emotions.

Fortunately, today I saw the change of mood for what it was. I took a step back and realised quickly that all systems have issues and in the big scheme of things it would get sorted. No lives were being threatened and there was no reason to spoil a beautiful sunny day. I did get on and calmly sort the issue, but I'm not superman (all the time). I did have a few hours where the feelings of frustration stayed with me. So I got on with some physical work in the garden to let off steam.

It gets better. Once you start to notice that your thoughts aren't who you are, it will take less and less time to get back to sailing again, so to speak. In my bad old days I used to be in these places for days and sometimes weeks. I'm sure the doctor would have prescribed pills for me, if I had ever thought to ask. Nowadays, at worst, I only spend a few hours lost in the thoughts that seem so real at the time, with my feelings ringing alarm bells for me to know that my thinking is – well, it's just off. Sometimes, just like today; I saw the thinking was so obvious and when the feelings started to hit me I knew exactly what it was about and didn't get involved with it – well, almost.

Your feelings barometer is helpful – very helpful – in living your life the way that feels best for you. And that's the point. The barometer is telling you about your direction.

It's telling you which way is your "True North". A lot of people chase around trying to find their life purpose or the meaning of their lives. To me, this is a lot of "head stuff", thoughts and intellect combining to lead you on a merry dance whilst ignoring your feelings barometer which is pointing you to your heart's desire all the time. It never stops. It always points true. It is totally reliable. That's the way it works, like Jack Sparrow's magic compass in that great movie *Pirates of the Caribbean*, it points to your heart's desire. Listen to me now, sounding like a teller of a fairy story; but it's true. Let me give you a couple more examples to demonstrate.

A little while back I did business with a man who, at face value, seemed like he was offering a huge opportunity. It was a big deal and it would transform my business activities. Everything in my head seemed to be saying, "Go for it", but somewhere else in me alarm bells were going off. The opportunity was too good to miss, I thought. So I shushed the bells and carried on. Three months later the man disappeared, leaving me with unpaid bills and debts to pay. Good news: it wasn't life threatening, but I should have listened to how I felt. My barometer was right all along!

Why did I write this book? You know, I couldn't tell you how it started. A lot of my older relatives started leaving this world and I could see how their great stories, histories of our time and wonderful life experiences, were being lost. I had a feeling. Around those times I wrote a journal, clearing my thoughts for the day or focusing on some aspect of my life.

That felt right for a while. Then it just got a bit like hard work and drudgery so I stopped that and started to write. I mean really write. Poetry and prose. At school I'd never done well in the arts and maybe that's why I didn't start long ago – I had something in my conditioning telling me "no", but this felt so right, and pretty soon the idea came to me to write a book. The book that nobody in my family had ever written. There was no decision to make. It just felt good – the writing, creating something of value. All good. Notice that I didn't think all this through, I didn't analyse and do a business plan.

What I do know is that I want to do this and the world will benefit from it in some way. I'm not sure how, but if only ONE reader gets their life-changing nugget from it then it will have all been worthwhile. I hope there will be a life-changing nugget for you here.

One last thing I must mention is what I call "phantom feelings". Often we'd love to know what is creating our feelings so that we can fix them. Truth is it's just part of being human. "I must know why I'm feeling like this" – that's the thought. But sometimes feelings relate to something much deeper than your conscious mind, so you may think that you are mad because someone hasn't emailed you back, but it could actually be something completely different; and you won't find out what that is by thinking about it.

When you get into some feeling that you think is telling you something, please give it a little time. If it's a "bad" feeling, one that hurts, best to let that feeling go and get back into a place of clarity first and foremost. Then you will be much more likely to see what the issue is. If it's a "good" feeling, love or compassion, that's easier to trust. If the good feeling continues, gets warmer and deepens, what could be better than that! My belief is that in human nature, good is the default setting for everyone.

Finally, back to your inner compass. You know that a compass doesn't tell you your destination, it just points in the right direction, moment to moment, so that you know where to head. It may not tell you your ultimate life's purpose, but if you trust it and follow it you will have a path to follow that is the most natural life for you to lead. In the end it's the sum of the experiences you have that give your life meaning. Job done!

And if you don't follow your compass that's okay, too. I didn't follow mine for years, as you know, but even those years, those experiences were useful for me later on. I'm sure that my most challenging moments were always accompanied by the feelings telling me my thinking was not good for me; it was all part of the action, though.

Often I didn't pay attention to the signs until it was too late. I realised that at some point and saw it as just the delusion it was. As time goes on I get fooled less often and when I do I see it so much more quickly. I get to live a much easier and more fulfilling life now I am back trusting its guidance, most of the time.

If you believe in something greater than all of us that is shaping everything that's happening: God, the universe, Universal Energy, call it what you will, then you have a unique and important part to play.

As in the Shakespeare quote that starts this book, we are in a huge production and we all have a part to play. In that big orchestra, making the most beautiful music called creation, we are just one note. An important note.

All you ever have to do is play your note, not someone else's, not as directed by something else, just your note. Pure and clear. It's not complicated. You know exactly how to do it. See it like that and life is so easy.

Working with your barometer and following your compass IS playing your note. For me that's how you do effortless living. I can't recommend it enough.

Finding Your A-Game

It's that moment when your chest feels like it's going to burst, or you sit in quiet beauty and feel totally at peace with yourself, or that warm comfortable moment under your covers at the start or end of the day when you just know that it's all good.

In those moments, you are really at peace with yourself, there are no decisions to make. Things are so clear that no thought is required on which option to take, which direction to head. You have time, space and all the clarity you need to do the perfect job, to live your best life.

These are great times, times when you know everything is going right, you are confident, great opportunities come at you thick and fast. It's a place full of energy, you have great ideas, you are creative and guess what? It's all coming off. You could call it luck, but you know deep down that it was all going to happen this way. All these situations are times when you are at your best, a place that sports psychologists and TV commentators call your "A-Game".

I'm guessing you noticed passages of this book where I was in that place, where gratitude filled me for what I feel and who I am in that moment. No affirmations or positive thinking required, thank you! I'm sure you've been like that, too – remember it? Isn't it wonderful?

When you're playing your A-Game you just can't lose!

Well, guess what? You can NEVER lose.

Oh, there are times when you feel like you are losing, like nothing is going your way, and then you drop onto the thought that it's all going to go horribly, permanently wrong. I'll bet you noticed a few times like that in my story as well.

I used to search, almost maniacally, for my holy grail. I called it the "elevator button". Consider, if that place I was in when I was on my A-Game was the penthouse of an impressive high-rise building: great views where you can see the sun and far into the distance, clear air, calm and impressive. Alternatively, in the lobby, it's crowded full of people, no sunlight and hard to make progress. I wanted to be able to step in the elevator and press the button for the top floor. Wouldn't you?

I found a few things that worked in my life like that elevator button: riding my bike, connecting with dear friends, making love, doing my tai chi practice, walking the dog or even reading a great novel. They all qualified, but nothing was reliable. Other times, just being with my partner had the opposite effect and it was only when I left the house to do something inane like drive down the motorway, that my elevator started to rise. If you find a reliable elevator button, be sure and let me know.

I guess we are only human and that means we have good times and bad, just like the rolling waves in the sea or the sun and rain in the springtime. Both occur together. The good news is that after the rain the sunshine returns. After the crest of the wave there is always the swell. Why is that good news? Because it means there's nothing to do. No elevator button required. If you find yourself in a bad place then know that if you just ride through it you'll be riding the crest of the wave again soon enough.

In my life I've sailed yachts in seas where the waves seemed, and sometimes were, way bigger than the boat. I wondered if we would capsize or be swamped, but the wave always passed magically under us. We even surfed off the crest of those waves with very little effort. It was magical. Your life is like that, too.

Have you ever had something you've really been dreading? Maybe it's your tax return deadline? Maybe there is some family or relationship issue that you are really worried about? Maybe it's a fear of failing or letting someone down? Think about an experience like this that you have had. How did it go for you? I'll bet it turned out much better than you expected, didn't it? Just like the yacht, your "wave" passed magically by and you coped with it much better than you thought possible. There! Aren't you amazing?

And all the stress you put yourself under before those situations, was it ever warranted? Don't our thoughts go nineteen to the dozen about everything that could happen, should, or shouldn't happen. My, we sometimes hold onto life hard in those situations. That's my experience, anyway.

Maybe you can train yourself. I think it was Lord Tennyson who said of finding motivation, "I sit down to write at 9.30 every day and my inspiration arrives at 9.35". You can bet that however talented a writer he was, Tennyson had his off days, just like the rest of us.

So there's something even bigger at play, a superpower we all have to hand available to us at all times. I call it the "B-Game".

Back to my TV commentators for a moment: if you were watching tennis on TV, you'd see a player hit a first serve and a second serve very differently. On the first serve he can give it everything and go for the win. That's the A-Game. If he misses, no biggie, he gets another go. The shot he makes on the second attempt, when he is under pressure and needs to work the percentages, is just as well played, but in a totally different way. It's his B-Game, perfect for the situation he's in and there to take him into a more positive place, a new serve where he can take a bigger risk, where he can go for the win once again.

You also have a B-Game. Do you know how significant this fact is?

At ALL times you have the capability and the resources you need. Your intuition never deserts you. Even when I was totally in the grip of my stories about the hunter-gatherer or being successful – total illusion as you know by now – I always had my B-Game to serve me.

Even when things don't feel like they are going well, you have at your disposal the ability to make the right decision, do the right thing and come through it better than you would ever have thought possible. Take today. As I write this I've had a torrid twenty-four hours. My personal values have been sorely tested and yet I've done business and done it well. I've written this piece and I'm very happy with it. In fact, it's the perfect moment for me to explain what's happening for right now. I hope you are enjoying it? Yes sir, the B-Game Rocks!

One thing to watch for, though: getting stuck in your B-Game. I wouldn't recommend it. Sometimes I think that playing the percentages is good. You get more wins than losses. But life gets really fun when you go for it, when you're in your A-Game and everything is going right. A great indicator for me is when I'm holding on too tight, really wanting things to happen and trying a bit too hard. That's when I realise I'm probably playing my B-Game.

The thing that works for me here is to relax, take it easy, just like the tennis player composing himself between games. Then I can come back fresh and see whether my A-Game has returned. It might not happen straight away, but I know that it will sooner or later and that's when life goes to a new level!

Just like a top professional sportsman, a star, you have your A-Game and your B-Game to serve you at all times. You are a complete player in the game of life. You are ready and fully able to ride the waves and the swell of life with no stress and with a sympathy for the prevailing weather that gets you to your destination every time. Know you are the captain of your own ship, one that's unsinkable, and when you trust that, you can be satisfied that whatever the weather, you've got it covered.

Little Nudges

This next insight is not so much a tool, it's about noticing signs around you and using that knowledge to guide you to your best life, to playing your note in a easy and clear way. Just like serendipity and seeing opportunities as they land at your feet, there are other signs out there for you. These signs usually come up when you are heading against the natural flow of life. You've heard of going with the flow, well this is the exact opposite. In the flow your A-Game is always to hand. When you are out of the flow it feels like you are always playing catch-up and your form is deserting you.

Have you ever been in a situation where you need a set of things to happen and they don't? Well, maybe everything happens for a reason. Maybe you are marching the wrong path and the implicate order is telling you just that.

Take my week this week. The first thing that happened to me was my foot swelled up overnight and in the morning I was hobbling badly. It was like I wasn't meant to travel, in a week when I was due in London. I can see you reading this and getting very cynical at this point. I would be, too, but life is a whole body experience, and my foot cleared up pretty quickly after the trip was done! I'd definitely agree that I was mad if two other things hadn't happened: first, I had booked a train weeks in advance to save money.

Good thinking eh? Except there were major flood warnings all over the UK the day I was booked. News bulletins recommended not travelling, but I soldiered on and made it to the station.

Electric lines came down, but still I made it down to London. I was going to do this trip and make the meetings I had organised! This was going to be a productive week, dammit!

There I go, controlling my life and paddling hard against the current. Even if you discount these events, these nudges, as being my warped imagination, there's more ...

I had booked three meetings in London. Good planning on my part. Effective use of time. Well, the first meeting didn't happen – a diary mix up. No problem, re-organised it for the next day and took a dinner engagement that I would have rather avoided. Just roll with it. I'm twisting and turning, paddling hard in the strong currents surrounding me. Enjoying the challenge of it, too! I can do this!

Then the meeting the next morning was sabotaged by a customer query that unearthed a fault in one of my products. Whilst digging for the solution to that issue I also found two others and fixed them. One step back to take two forward, I told myself. Half way through the next meeting another customer had a major technical issue. Life or death, they said! Well, that nixed my meeting and spoiled the next while I tried to find a wifi connection and sort out "Armageddon". I did my job calmly and patiently, and the person I was meant to meet was very understanding, too. And then it struck me ...

Both my sympathetic friend and I were struggling with our lives in that moment, trying to get somewhere. Do you get a sense now that it's not just a coincidence? That there were too many things that just weren't going right?

Maybe you're thinking that I'm incompetent or just plain dumb. Actually I am just misguided. Misguided by myself. As Jane Austen said:

"We all have a better guide in ourselves, if we would attend to it, than any other person can be."

I could have done things the easy way, but I chose to do it my way "come hell or high water". I did a bit of both and got the job done, despite a lot of nudges that I should be doing something different.

Am I down or low at this point? Hell NO! This is just life. Sometimes it's hard and sometimes it's beautifully easy. I don't need to describe to you some of the wonderful highs that I've experienced because you've read them already. Actually, I got a lot of good things done, but it could have been a lot easier. I could have done without hobbling around London for starters! Okay, it's clear to me now: I should have played this week very differently.

Think about people you know who have been struck down with major illnesses. Heart attacks and cancer. I bet you know a few, some quite close to you, maybe. I know it's a complicated world that we live in but maybe some of us, including me, have been ignoring those nudges and we just get bigger nudges until we are knocked flat and are forced to make a change to our lives. You might say this is nonsense, but maybe it's worth stopping to consider? It might just be good for your health.

Stand back a moment. This concept of nudges might be harder to believe, but it fits beautifully with serendipity. Serendipity offers you the chance to take the opening doors that just appear. Nudges give you fantastic signs to take another course. What a guidance system you have around you! All you have to do is follow the signs. Not only do you have an inner compass, but you get signposts, too!

At this point you might be thinking, "How can I do this when I have a specific goal or ambition to achieve?" In my book, having the intention is great – used the right way it means you'll be looking for the right opportunities – but being open to all the guidance that's available will keep you in the flow. So if you are getting guidance and you don't follow it, it's your lookout. Maybe your desired outcome is not going to happen for you, but if you allow a little serendipity into your life, there will be something even better for you. As Mum used to say:

"Something good will come of this."

Now, I'm not a fatalist. I don't believe that everything is signed and sealed, no point in wearing a seatbelt. But if you believe David Bohm, Joe Jaworski, Marcus Bach and me, maybe you can navigate life in an easier, more natural way than you are doing at the moment. That's certainly the case for me. It's something I am doing better these days – put all these tools together and you'll definitely play your note, clear and true. When you do that, you are there, living on purpose, with meaning – effortless, as Michael Neill would say.

Here's what would a perfect flow day would look like for me:

I'm free. In the clear. Nothing around me holding me back. I could do anything now, be anything. My chest expands and I breathe, free and easy. My heart is filling me up. I'm ready for the world.

I look around. Which way to step out? The world is my oyster and I am a servant of the world. I get up ready to start the day. Command me, oh world!

What next? There's some stuff that comes to mind. It's the dross, taking care of business. Not important – urgent maybe – but it's not going to change my life or anyone else's for the better. So what is important? If I'm not careful I could get drawn into it. I could get frustrated that no great ideas are coming up for me. I just wait patiently or I gently start something to give me something to flow with. Like a sailboat, once under way you can feel for the wind.

And then, without any thinking about it, something comes to me; love moves me to care for you, the reader, first and foremost. In loving you I feel the wonderful fullness of me. Passion bids me write of the wonders of the world and share the truth of my life with others. Gratitude inspires me to contact people who I will help today. There are no conditions to my actions. I do it with no requirement for me. If I just do all this, and walk the dog in the fresh air, it will be another great day.

I know how good I feel when I eat well, too. The energy of my physical being powers my soul, my vigour, my strength, my intention. That puts me in the right place today, tomorrow and every day.

When I do all this, the world arrives at my feet. Opportunities jump up to meet me. They meet and match my realisations and insights to create something good. When I forget to live like this, I'm sure to see that I'm off track and stop, chill out and start again.

When the path opens up like this, strangers become friends, friends become community. Community has resilience, has a powerful energy for creating a beautiful world for me and for all of us. I follow and I lead at the same time, an integral part of the dance. Who cares exactly where it leads? I lift my face to the sky and laugh. What could be better than this?

And in the cool of the evening I hold my love close. I stroke her face and feel my love pour into her, as hers pours into me. Our talk is inconsequential, but our nearness is special, divine even. Making love is the natural expression of us in this sacred place. It's the ultimate magic that sprinkles over an already perfect day. This is the life I love and life loves me. And that's all there is to it – simple.

Reason, Season or Lifetime

It occurs to me that all through this story I had some amazing people in my life. People who helped me see things more clearly and know what felt right for me in my life, so that I made decisions and took action in a way that really suited me, with real clarity and peace of mind.

Let me give you an example. For almost two years I lived with two beautiful young kids who yearned for their dad. He was in my life for a reason. I was never sure what he wanted. In some ways he wanted to know them and be their father. In others it seemed not. It seemed hard for them, and consequently hard for us all. Now, I don't pass any judgement on them and their relationship, but I do know that he held up an imaginary mirror for me to see myself as a father.

This was at a time when I wasn't living with my kids. By leaving home, a year earlier, I'd broken the relationships that I had with them and started new ones. This gave me the perfect opportunity to appreciate my own children more and to know how I wanted them to be treated, how I wanted them to know me. This mirror was priceless.

There was one time when Ben, my son, rang me asking to meet. I arranged to drive down that very night and have dinner with him. It was a five hour round trip, but I knew that just to spend a couple of hours with him, in person, was important for both of us. I don't think we said much that was very meaningful at dinner, but we both got something from being together in those moments. The mirror really worked for me then.

Another way B's ex-husband helped me was with the way he treated her. There was another mirror, showing me how people perceive each other, through what were probably innocent actions, or at worst just two people who had once been together, but were now travelling different paths.

As I looked in this mirror it showed me how I could be seen to be treating my wife. We were separated at this point and it made me very careful. I still cared for her – after all, we'd been together for so long. Youngsters, Man and Wife, Mum and Dad. That was too deep a relationship not to honour. Even though I was a problem to her because she loved me and wanted me still, I saw B's ex and knew how I would respect that relationship. It felt right to do that.

My dad: he was a wonderful mirror for me – still is. After all, he's here for my lifetime. He showed me how a father and a son have ties. They set expectations through innocence and love. As a father you want to be proud of your son. As a son you want your father to be proud of you. It's those simple things, yet how significant they seem.

There was a downside to this, though. Thoughts of obligations, criticisms and judgements. These are difficult things to bear, on both sides. They don't help me with peace and satisfaction, but it's good to see that, the innocent mistake that it is. When you see that's all it is, that changes everything!

And B, my loving partner for eight wonderful seasons, was also a great mirror for me. She was slow and present in life, when I was busy and distracted. She went with the flow when I tried to control life. She let her emotions out into the world, just when I bottled mine up and tried harder. This was huge for me. It let me see how I acted and helped me tremendously, to understand how I wanted to show up in the world. It turns out that I only saw that clearly once that mirror was broken.

I guess some lessons come to us in different ways. What I saw in that mirror has made a huge and positive change to the way I live my life. I'm so grateful for that.

It's clear to me now that Lucy, my wife, is with me for a lifetime. We met as kids and have been together through thick and thin and very thin. Somehow the rope that was our connection frayed to the last strand but endured. It has been a deep and abiding grounding in my life and I pay tribute to her here for letting me go on my journey, for being the one who kept what little of our connection remained, alive.

When you repair a rope the join becomes the strongest part, and just in that way, both of our journeys have helped us make our connection one of the deepest and most nourishing parts of my life experience. It's like that old saying: I could take on the world from this place.

Whenever you're critical of anybody else, it's not the other people doing anything to you – you are just seeing yourself. If you don't like what you see, it's your problem, not theirs.

"Judge not, that ye be not judged"

Matthew 7:13

An old quote from the Bible, this came to me again and again during the two years I was on my journey. It sang to me loud and clear. When I was judging someone else, I was seeing me in the mirror they were holding for me. If I didn't like what I saw then there was something for me to see and know about myself.

As you've already read, most of the time I saw that as opportunity. Sometimes it did turn out to be quite challenging for me, but I knew there was learning in there and that I'd get it one day, if not right then.

More than that, if others were judging me, I knew I was holding up a mirror for them. I've got a friend whom I have always encouraged. In fact I take it upon myself to be encouraging with my friends. I want them to do well – wouldn't you? It turns out that this guy always thought I was bullying him. Wow, what a difference in perception!

Whenever that happens, you are holding up a mirror for them and they are seeing something for themselves. I could be worried about that. The last thing I would ever want to do is upset a friend, but the truth is that I didn't upset him, he saw himself and that's what upset him. In that place I can feel compassion for my friends, because they are my friends and I still want them to do well.

Everyone is in your life, and you are in theirs, for a reason; sometimes it is for a short while and sometimes you are linked by birth or some deeper connection. I'd like to think that everyone I value as a friend, a true friend, is with me for a lifetime. Is that just me? I know that one of the five top regrets of the dying is that they didn't keep in touch with friends.

I have people in my life whom I haven't seen for many years, but I know with absolute certainty that they'll come back into my life at some point, and it will be like carrying on where we left off. So lifetime isn't a prison sentence – it's a gift, if we can be open to it.

Beautiful Minds

Let's continue this focus on people and talk about relationships for a moment. We all think we have relationships with other people, but let me tell you that in every relationship you think you have, you have three relationships.

Dr Dicken Bettinger once told me that there are no relationships. He says that the only relationship you ever have is with yourself. For me, just like the mirrors I spoke of earlier, it's all about how you see it ...

First, there is your relationship with yourself. When I'm in a good place I can listen to someone deeply and properly, creating the connection that energises us both. I can be loving, too. Wow, what a gift that is! And when I'm not in a good place? I personally tend to detach and shut down, the script, my stories, my habitual thinking tells me that the other person wouldn't want to know me like this and why should I inflict myself on them?

It seems that my partner wants more physical contact, comforting and supporting. That's great when I'm in a good and loving place, but hard to do if I'm not. The first thing to be clear on is looking after you. Then you can be ready to do the rest.

One thing to be really careful about is trying to help someone when they are not in a good place. You know you want to, but my experience is that often they bring you down into your thinking, and that's not good. In the early days with B, even when our relationship was fresh and new, somehow, a number of times, we dragged each other down and in that double dark place where all you see are shadows and insecurities, we said things that would have split us up if we had really believed what we were saying.

So look after number one first. You owe it to everyone to do that.

The second is the relationship you have with the other person. Are you careful to connect with them? I mean properly, by listening deeply for their feeling. Of course, if this is a loved one, this is actually the best thing ever. The connection is easy. I mean, that's probably why you were attracted to each other in the first place.

Add to that listening to them, I mean really listening, and that connection will have huge power. Love flows and in that place you'll feel unbelievable intimacy and sharing, without even touching them. Of course a cuddle doesn't go amiss here, unless it's your dad or your son. Hold on, come to think of it, why not cuddle them?

While you're in that place it's not all about a feeling. It's about understanding too. Understanding their wants and needs, wishes and dreams, because knowing them, really knowing them is vitally important, as you are about to see. Not only does this deepen your connection beautifully, it gives you important information so that when you aren't speaking or physically together, you know them.

Get the connection and the understanding right and you can still feel them, even when you are thousands of miles away. Who says we need phones or email when we are all connected? No, I'm not mad. Try feeling for your partner or a loved one next time you are apart from them and you'll get something – it might take a little practice to listen inside for them, but it works, trust me.

The last way a relationship works is that you take your understanding and carry on what can become a fictitious relationship. When you are away from them a lot or you don't speak when you really should, you end up having the conversation with them in your head, deciding things on their behalf and moving on, doing things based on those decisions. And there's the potential danger.

The other person actually knows nothing about this conversation. If you are lucky – and this is what you'd like to happen – your understanding is really good. You've been listening to them properly and know them really well and when you do meet up, whatever you decided turns out to be on the money. No problem.

But what if you got it wrong and it's not what they want or how they'd want you to be? What happens when you've not been really listening for a while and you've decided lots of things, in a way that you think will be good for them, is that those decisions are based on equally fictitious assumptions you've previously made. Uh OH! Danger is looming large. WATCH OUT!

You think you are doing well by them, but you couldn't be farther from the truth. I'm sure this mistake, made so innocently in the interests of the relationship, happened to me. Another HUGE lesson!

I can see the warning signs now and I make sure that I'm having a real relationship with the people I care about. Besides, that's where the connection is at its best and I have the deepest feelings for them. That's the greatest place on Earth – in my book! Call me an old softie, but I bet that deep down you feel the same way.

And if you do get into a place where you suspect that either or both of you are in danger of falling foul of fiction and entering into a melodrama, then that's the time to seek out great folk like Dicken B. He'll get you realising that it's all your thinking, and nobody else's. Like he said, there is really only one relationship you need to worry about – the one with yourself! And that means each of you. Then you'll be back on safe ground pretty quick.

Why don't we laugh more?

You know, that genuine big grin smile leading to a welling up of joy and a vocal, physical outpouring of mirth. If you're really lucky it might even lead to tears and the kind of uncontrollable laughter that has you struggling to breathe, unable to stop yourself. When did you last have that? Don't you feel great in those moments? My daughter, Helen, is so good at laughing, that unique kind of splitting-your-sides laughing.

I've been taught to be adult. It's in the script I follow, although less and less nowadays. If I find something funny I can just hold it in or smile wryly to myself so that nobody sees. Not good.

Maybe you don't even allow yourself to get that far? Or worse still, you scowl and tut at anyone who seems to be having fun. I've done that, too.

I guess it was all part of holding onto life too hard. Worrying about bills coming through the letterbox, how the kids were doing in school, or maybe for you it's worrying whether your partner is about to dump you?

Stop ... stop ... stop ...

OK, you're in deep, but just a simple laugh will take you some place richer, will free your spirit and turn a hard life into something wonderful. A ray of sunshine appearing out of the gloom. It's always there for you and in a moment your life can feel very different.

Where did that gloom come from? Truth is, you created it. Do you really know that any of your worries: bills, kids, girlfriends, have any truth to them? You don't. They might seem real to you, but let me compliment you on your vivid imagination. Because that's all it is.

So here's an idea: use that great imagination for something else. Why not dream a bit, of everything you could be, how great your kids are, how much you feel for your partner. How does that feel? How easy is it to smile from that place, and a smile leads to laughter, and suddenly, sunshine.

I could tell you about the physiology of laughing, how many muscles it activates, what chemicals your brain produces and how that makes you feel. I'm sure all that happens, but all I know is that there is nothing like a real, genuine laugh. Welling up from deep inside you and entering the world. Go on, laugh out loud! Even better, share it with a friend, see how that makes them feel, and you, too. It's the best! Money can't buy that.

Take one of the guys on the Pamplona trip. He was going through an acrimonious divorce and was very focused on his business, too. A serious situation. If you heard his stories you'd definitely agree. You know what? He can see the lightness in life. On our trip he laughed the most of anyone. It was a pleasure to be with him. Don't tell me it's too difficult, because it's not.

I could also tell you famous stories about people like Victor Frankl, who survived the concentration camps of World War Two because of his attitude. It's the ultimate proof that it's not about your circumstances. Go look him up, it's an inspiring read:

Man's Search for Meaning. How could anyone create camps like that? But then what fantastic lessons in life did the survivors get? I believe Herr Frankl was one of the few who talked about it openly, but one of many who lived very different lives after they'd realised who they really were.

You may be saying to yourself that it's hard to get started, but that's not true. Even reading this and being more aware of the fun and laughter that is all around you will take you there.

When you find a smile on your lips, don't hold back – let it turn into a chuckle. A proper laugh won't be far behind. You'll feel good about it, and then it will start to become part of everyday life. You'll have that sunshine more and more because you enjoy it so much.

Could it be that simple? Could you make your life totally different without changing any of your circumstances?

I'm betting that once you've started listening to your feelings barometer and trusting that you've got all the skills you need to play your note, you're going to see the world a little bit more lightly. Because life is just a game and you are an expert player right from the word go. Hopefully you are starting to see that as you've been reading.

There are times when I've taken life far too seriously – in fact, a lot of my life, when I wasn't following my compass, when I thought that life was a game I could lose, when success was something that I had to attain. I just had to win the backgammon game! I had to! Even as I was doing my learning about this new way of being and finding me, I'd be earnest and passionate about getting what I was being taught.

I must mention a fantastic lady called Rita Shuford. She was supporting a crowd of us at one particular event and I was doing my thing: must learn it, must get it. Every time I did this, there was Rita smiling broadly at me and wagging here finger as if to say, "Take it lightly, boy!" And that's how all those folks who've been living this way for years show up in the world. Full of lightness and so much more open to life.

Even I have started to see it that way. Today I was caught on the motorway for four hours, missing my flight to see my dad. Those two things could have caused me serious sense of humour failure, but I was fine. Then I got to the airport to get another ticket, had to go to another terminal in a short amount of time. Hassled by the security staff (who where only doing their job, I might add) I made it to the gate without having had a drink or been to the toilet for six hours; my bag spilt its contents twice on the way.

Maybe I shouldn't be taking this trip. Remember the nudges? With all these things making it difficult for me I could have been mad. Instead I had a laugh with the flight attendants and serendipity started to take charge. Maybe it was because I could tell the story with a smile and a joke, when some people might be fuming and stressed by now. They gave me a better seat and something to eat to keep me going. At this point I'd made it through to get where I wanted to go – to see my dad. Worth it, I reckon and I'm still happy I did it. Only a little nudge, honestly.

If you aren't convinced that living a lighter life is available to you, let me tell you about St Francis Hospice in Berkhampstead, UK. It was my mum's last home and boy, was it a great place. I was surprised. It's a place of death and sorrow, but it felt much more like a place of happiness and peace. Part of this was down to the wonderful, caring staff.

While Mum was there they held a wedding for the daughter of a patient who was terminally ill, but still hanging in there. All these people were really making the most of their time together. Really taking the most from life. I've seen more research that the top regret of the dying is that they didn't live their lives more like that – as they wanted to live, rather than how they were expected to.

Why wait? Start living a lighter life. One of joy and lightness. Start as soon as you like. You've got all the tools, skills and knowledge right inside you, right now.

Behind You!

Have you ever been to a good old-fashioned pantomime where the "baddie" always makes their entrance by trying to creep up on our hero? It's our job, as the audience, to shout and holler:

"He's behind you!"

To which our hero turns in the wrong direction and asks:

"Where is he? I don't see anything"

We shout even louder and laugh. All part of a fun Saturday matinee. Great stuff. Your purpose, genius or passion is like that. I know it's no "baddie", far from it! Just like the pantomime character it's hiding right there in the open, where everyone can see it, and you are the one turning, turning and asking, "Where?"

Have you ever felt like that?

Maybe you have seen a real life magician − it might have been entertainment at a party. You know it's magic, a clever trick of deception or sleight of hand, but you can't figure it out for the life of you − until you see him doing the trick with someone else and see that he's getting their attention to move there so that he can do something over here. "That's how he does it", you sigh. All part of the entertainment, the glamour of the evening.

Fascinating isn't it?

The point is that our genius is hiding in plain sight or the trick is being performed right in front of your nose. It's right there for you, all the time. It always was there. It always will be there. All you have to do is spot it. Think of all the energy you've spent asking, "Where?" and turning, turning. It's like looking for your car keys. The more you look, the more they elude you! You are the hero on your stage. "It's behind you!" One of life's great jokes, don't you think? Laugh with me and we'll both enjoy the panto!

Maybe some of the advice your friends keep offering you is great advice because they can see the trick you are playing on yourself. But they're your friends. "They mean well, but what do they know?" you say to yourself. Quite often they can see something that you don't quite. They might not give you the feedback quite right, but maybe it's worth taking a moment to step back and see if you can see what's right in front of you. Don't you think?

The best coach I know spends most of her time biting her lip, hard, to restrain herself from telling her clients what she sees for them so easily. In my opinion that's one of the two great qualities of a coach: seeing what's right in front of the other person's nose. The other great quality is the ability to create a space for her clients where they get to see it for themselves. They get the insight and after that, life is different! Now that, in my opinion, is worth paying for!

But if you don't have a coach there are a few things that might work for you. After all, what you are looking for is hiding in plain sight.

First, life is a whole body experience. You'll be somewhere, doing something and you will suddenly feel full of energy. Remember being in love for the first time? There you go, you have experienced it! Or maybe you'll get a headache or a pain somewhere. No, it's not just that you should be wearing your glasses or sitting properly. Your body is giving you a sign. It's funny how we don't think this stuff is important – it is. Louise Hay's book sold thirty eight million copies for good reason. So when your body tells you something, take note, look around. There's something there for you.

Second, look on the edges of your vision, not at what is right in front of you. Just like the magician's trick. Often the thing that's right in front of you, your job or business, your everyday busy life, is the diversion and if you just look at what else is going on there is something there for you to see. You'll get the knack for this more and more as you naturally widen your vision of your life, when you follow your compass.

Third, think back to your childhood. Those times that you might now think of as naive, now that you've taken on all the conditioning that adulthood brings. Think of the things you loved to do as a kid. The things that made you feel really good, especially if you stopped doing them and don't really remember why, are parts of your life that you haven't taken advantage of in your adulthood.

It may sound like I'm asking you to change the way you live your life or try harder, but that would just be looking for the car keys again. The best thing to do is just carry on living and the car keys will turn up, like magic! I hope that just reading this is enough –

enough to jog your memory, to raise your awareness, to remember the true you. If you don't see anything right here, right now, then watch for it over the coming days and weeks. It will be there.

Once you see it more clearly, your genius, your purpose, your note, then a new and richer life opens up for you. You start to feel the beautiful harmony of playing with the biggest symphony out there. It just feels so right and in that moment, in every moment, you hear that music, the music in you. You are everything you ever could be. Wonderful!

Lest We Forget

On the 11th hour of the 11th day of the 11th month everywhere in the UK there is a remembrance service going on. Whatever town I'm in I always go to the local service. It's important to remember – remember all the people who died in the wars. It's an important warning to us all about what humanity can be capable of. An unfortunate truth.

Thirty years ago, I played the last post to the assembled crowd. Then the priest recited those famous words, "We will remember them". It was a moment of reflection and an important minute's silence. The stillness was powerful. It still is today.

My parents were only young in the Second World War, but my grandparents had been alive through both world wars. Their experience of life, their losses and their memories were strong, enough for them to furrow their brows at the thought of what they'd been though, friends and family they'd lost. It was all very real to them and I saw that. It made it real for me, too.

My grandparents are gone now and there are few people around to keep those memories alive, to keep the awareness going. The great news is that the services are still well attended by new generations. Boy and Girl Scouts, school children and, unfortunately, war widows of younger generations. Despite all this effort to remember, we keep forgetting!

And there it is, another fundamental quality of being human – we forget. Even in this case, when things are highly organised across the nation, when we are trying our hardest to remember.

We still make decisions and lives are lost. It's a shame, but true.

What if?

What if we had a remembrance day to remember all the great things about the world, all the happy little and big events that happen every day. Acts of kindness and love. Genuine moments of affection and compassion. It seems to me that these come and go, hardly noticed. Just like Bob Cratchit in *A Christmas Carol*, that famous novel by Charles Dickens, kindness endures despite all Scrooge's attempts to squash or smother Bob's good intentions.

That famous novel is all about remembering, and in that place, knowing that humans have kindness built in to our makeup. For some reason we don't seem to focus on it. Instead we focus on problems, intent on fixing them, or we worry about the future, intent on creating a good life for us and our loved ones, or steering and controlling our friends and children, to help them live well. It's far too easy to get focused on the fixing, the worrying and the controlling, and what is life like then? I know it. I did it!

Let's remember all the good stuff. Let's have a national day once a year to really celebrate the happiness and good fortune that is here for us all. Let's smile, shake hands, laugh, hug and live that day remembering that it's all good – really!

Now look at each of us as individuals. We, too, forget. We get caught up in the business of life, things happen, we react and respond. When do we stop? In this modern life it seems to me that we just get ever busier. We forget our dreams in the face of all the things that seem like they have to be done. We don't get the time to use our talents or do the things we love, just because there's too much to do and our dreams get pushed to the bottom of the to-do list. And you know what happens then.

Even when you are playing at life with your B-Game and your feelings barometer is helping you find your way through the twists and turns there is one thing that is even more powerful and important for you – remembering and being you.

This morning, as I was confronted by the task list of my day, I did one very important thing: I remembered how I love to write and made sure that it wasn't pushed to the bottom of the pile. It's what I love. It's what I was inspired to do. In writing this piece for you I am clear, at peace and I know it is what I was here to do today. That really means a lot to me.

Being you is what it's all about! There can be no better way to live.

What about all the things that need doing? Sure, they will get done, but you and I are not just here to operate the machinery of life, are we? We are the designers and players of the game called Life. We roll the dice, new possibilities appear and we use our wisdom and inspiration to make our moves. All these moves, ours and everyone else we are connected to, are what make up life. It's the big crazy game we all play, as B used to say.

Being you is when you have fun playing that game. When you are playing it someone else's way, how much fun is that? See my point?

How do you remember? Well, some people do it on their holiday or vacation, when they have a bit of room to breathe and reconnect with themselves. Some do it on the golf course. Some drive their favourite road. Conditions might not be the best, but that doesn't stop them being in that place where their thinking and worries clear. Maybe you meditate, practice tai chi or just grow plants in your garden. Whenever your thoughts clear you are there, right there.

When your mind is still, new ideas bubble up to get you excited about taking that next step in your life, the one that is uniquely yours. In this place your feelings barometer will be telling you that all is good. It's a wonderful knowing. You'll have your A-Game back, although you never really lost it, and you'll be ready to meet life at your best again.

It's not just important for nations to remember what can happen if they are not careful. It's not just a once a year thing. Remembering is for you to connect with yourself, to see once more what makes you excited about life and to have your talents to hand. Just be you. It's a priceless gift. Nobody else on Earth can be that. You are marvellous and unique. For that reason alone it's worth remembering every day, even if it's just for a few minutes ...

... Be you ...

That's all there is to it.

Taking Care of Business

There once was a guy called Abraham Maslow. He created something that's commonly known as Maslow's hierarchy of needs. Everyone who's ever explained it to me starts at the bottom of the pyramid where you have basic physical needs, like breathing, eating and sleeping. Apparently these have to be satisfied before you can live in any more meaningful way – and that's how a lot of us live our lives. Where's the next meal coming from? How do I pay the bills? Financial security is the next level of the Maslow's triangle. But let me tell you about the top of Mr M's ascension. He called it self-actualisation.

When you live at that pinnacle of life, you are at peace with whatever comes. You have no need to express yourself, you just are you. The Buddhists might call this Nirvana. Maslow took a more scientific approach and interviewed twenty one people who he thought were at their pinnacle, so he could describe that place in life that isn't so tangible, but is literally the peak of existence. If you believe Mr M's model that is ...

And there's the rub. I'm not the first to notice this, but some of the qualities that Maslow described for self-actualised people would exist regardless of their circumstances. Gandhi was himself regardless of whether he was a successful lawyer or fasting in protest or sharing his life with people in his country. It's wasn't food that fed him, literally! For me he was a shining example of someone who lived his life from that pinnacle. He stood on the summit of his life and admired the view. It might have been stony and barren in places but it was uniquely him.

Come back to every day life with me now. We aren't all Gandhi, are we? But could it be possible for us all to live our lives from our pinnacle? What if you came at life from the place of "this is me, just me, it's who I am and what I bring to the world"?

You might argue that it couldn't possibly happen like that because there is always business to take care of. What's that old saying? "Only two things are certain in life: death and taxes." Perhaps that's why accountants and lawyers do so well! Or let's consider that old question of pragmatism: does the end justify the means or the means justify the end?" See, there's lots of perceived wisdom about how to live life in this, dare I call it, mundane way. Could there be another way for all of us?

I used to think that it's all right when you've got money and everything you need in life, but what I've found is that you can climb the hierarchy, just as Maslow lays it out, and still not make it to the top! To me, having more money, stuff, etc. feels like having a bigger mountain to climb – and it's not about climbing a mountain, it's about knowing that the mountain is yours and you can be at the summit whenever you want. Like a Himalayan Sherpa whose clients climb Everest as a once in a lifetime experience when the Sherpa has been many times. It's all about how you see it.

I know that when I show up as me, the real true me, and I play my note, surprising things happen. I meet great people who nourish me as I connect with them. Opportunities arise that I could never have planned. When I just punch the meal ticket and earn some money there's little joy to be had.

Okay, you could argue that living life balancing your triangle on its point is very unstable, but what could be easier than playing your note, just doing what you do best and living how feels most natural? Your note is built into you from birth, from conception. It's right there for you, and all you have to do is play.

So whenever you feel like you are toiling away deep in the mines of your mountain, STOP! Remember to just be you. Listen to your note as you start to play it again, loud and clear, then you just can't go wrong – and what a relief that is – you just can't go wrong!

"Strike a pose there's nothing to it."

Madonna

Life Beyond Money

I bet you've been wondering when I would get to this. Oh, how I've been looking forward to writing about it, too. Money has always been in my life. From my early years doing jobs so that I could earn a little money to go down to the toyshop and have that moment where I could buy something that I'd dreamt of, coveted even, for weeks.

I didn't choose the title of this book. I was on that great course held by that dynamic duo Richard Wilkins and Liz Ivory, called Broadband Consciousness. It's the place where I first told my jewellery story, the piece that you read in the introduction. After I told that story, Liz suggested the title to this book and I just knew it was right. There was no decision to make. Money has been the game I've played pretty much all my life. A lot of the time I got lost in that game and it felt like my reality.

It's like when you are driving and get taken in by the speed you're going. I'm not really sure why we all speed – it's breaking the law, after all, but here in the UK it's common practice, even when it's thought to be putting us in danger. Maybe speed feels good. I bet we've all seen how fast we can go, just for the thrill of it. Maybe you've got somewhere to get to and sooner is better than later. Could it be that everyone is going at speed so you do the same? Money is just the same.

Some people make money, just for the hell of it. They rack up a big number – more than they could ever spend – and it makes them feel good. People think they have to make an amount quickly and a lot of us see what everyone else has and "keep up with the Joneses". But money is not just about speed or seeing how fast you can go.

One time I was driving my family back from a holiday, on the Queens Highway, and I realised we were running low on fuel. I didn't know where the next fuel station was, but I had roughly calculated that we could make it. As the fuel gauge went down towards zero the others in the car started getting worried that we'd run out and be stranded by the roadside. They tried to persuade me to take a detour and find fuel. But where would that be? I was in the driving seat and I drove on in a kind of grim silence. We did miles in that silence with the gauge showing empty when we should have been enjoying the journey. Even I started to get worried. Had I got my calculations wrong? Was there something wrong with the gauge? See, even I got thinking, but you know what? We made it. I had been right all along. Why all that worry? We should have just trusted that everything was ok, but for some reason we didn't.

I know people who drive their car close to empty all the time and don't get worried. I know people who keep their car filled up to the brim, and everywhere in between. It's amazing how we can all think differently about how much we need – how much fuel or how much money.

For me, I wanted to be the best driver. Fastest yet safest, the most accredited and yet fuel conscious driver. I got lost in that ambition. It drove me! Like it says in that great book by Robert Kiyosaki, *Rich Dad Poor Dad*, I reached a stage where going fast in life, having everything going on, meant I needed lots of money and I had to go even faster to get it. Kiyosaki calls it the hamster wheel and I was there, enjoying driving that wheel round faster and faster. Never mind that it might be a bit tiring! Mastering the hamster wheel was everything.

Kiyosaki proposes a way to get off the wheel, a strategy that will have you producing enough money through other means to exceed your needs. It worked for him; but for me it's not about whether you are on a wheel at all. In fact, I'd suggest that if you've got that belief then get another one, one that's more helpful.

Did I ever have no money? I mean absolutely not a brass farthing to call on? No. In fact I had debt. It's like having money, but different. I could spend more as long as I could service the loans. Now that's a game within a game! So I have never REALLY gone without. Have you? I remember a big lesson when I gave up corporate life and the pay cheques stopped coming. The money just came more irregularly and I had to flex to fill the spaces. It was just a different way of thinking about and managing money.

So how much money do you need? Your answer to that might be: when I've paid off my cards or paid off my mortgage; "only seventeen years to go", or retired with that little cottage in France. Those are all thoughts or dreams that you might get just a bit too attached, too. Why wait for the day, driving in your own grim silence? Today is right here for you.

Maybe a better approach is to stop worrying about it. I know people with lots of money who are really worried about not having enough. They'd have a fuel depot behind their house, maybe just far enough away to upset the neighbours, but which is guaranteed unlimited supply. Would they ever use it all? I'm pretty sure the answer is "no". Then what happens when you are gone? Too late! A nice nest egg for your family, maybe. Could it be better to enjoy the benefits of the money while you are still alive?

I also know people who won't leave home for fear of using fuel, or speed insanely regardless of the cost in fuel and potentially to themselves, too. Like that great leader, Shackleton, they ration themselves to the very minimum and hope what they've got will last. A kind of self imposed famine. What kind of life is that? I'd love everyone to experience the abundance that life has to offer. Wouldn't you prefer a land of milk and honey to forty years in the wilderness, searching?

Everyone has a different thought about money and none of them are true. They just live in the reality they created, like I have been.

I remember biking with a guy who always travelled at 170 mph. As I was doing 70-80 mph, mildly speeding I know, he sped past me. Some time later on the same journey he sped past me again. He had to stop to fill up at least once more than I did, so did he get home much quicker but at double or treble the cost? He was risking being imprisoned straight off at those speeds. More importantly, he was risking his life! Amazing how we sometimes don't take the potential risk to ourselves into account, isn't it? His choice, I suppose and if it gave him the best experience who's to argue? We all have a choice how to live, after all.

The one thing I found out in the pursuit of speed, or money, is that I became so focused on the road ahead, on going as fast as I could – without taking too much risk, but fast fast fast – that I was completely missing the view. My experience of life was almost completely related to the needles on the instruments in front of me. Looking at it now I still get transfixed on my needles, my bank balance. I've been on expensive holidays and might as well not have been there, I was so far from present. I missed being at school plays and other unique events that I could have shared with my family. In fact, I don't regret it – I thought I was doing the right thing, playing the money game to "bring home the bacon", as the old saying goes. And how did playing the game serve me?

I live in an era of the global financial collapse, when pensions were devalued a long time ago and unless you have a LOT of money it's just something that you'll continue to deal with as your life goes on. Even if you have a big sum of money, you're probably working and worrying to protect it. You've still got to deal with it, but in other ways. Que sera sera!

Richard Wilkins had his big realisation when he went from "millionaire to there", as he calls it. In actual fact, "there" meant bankrupt, but it showed him that he still had life and he could still feel good about it. That feeling doesn't cost a penny. Nowadays he shares that message with everyone he can.

Recently I met a guy who's making good money, great money even, but realises now that it all pales into insignificance compared to feeling good, and making others feel good, too. In fact, he could see how badly he treated himself and the people around him before he got this new perspective: that you have everything you need and the game is just, well, a game.

If I look back, I see that the reason for my journey was to realise that I'd got lost in my game. Way too lost! I'm sure now that it was an innocent mistake, a delusion. I wanted to do well by everyone, for everyone and the strategy I knew was to work hard and persevere. Head down and graft. I used to tell my kids that one of our superpowers as a family was the ability to work hard. And it was hard. Where did it take me? Into the darkness.

I went on my journey and remembered who I am, but bizarrely I started playing the old way for B. I so wanted my new life to work and I guess I knew that the old ways would work – at least financially, as if that were all there was to life. When did I get deluded again? I don't know, but it was in the break-up with B that I really finally got it. I can have love in my life every day. It's not dependent on the money at all. Losing her was a huge price to pay, but in exchange I got an even bigger lesson that shows me how my life can really be for me, and how I can be with everyone I care about. That is what I call real wealth.

The really important thing is living – life beyond money – that's where the juice, the joy, the real experience is to be had. That's why there is only one section in this whole book about it. Oh, I get caught up in the game, but I see it much more for what it is. I choose not to let it define me.

The Impatience of Youth

You've joined me on part of my journey and seen the tumbledown road and the wild wood that was my thinking. I'm guessing you might have wanted to fast forward over that bit? In the old days I would, too. "Where's the meat?" I'd ask. I'd wait a bit longer, but then give up. Impatient. Yes, I was. Still am, I guess. I so believed that life was a destination and completely forgot to enjoy the journey.

That's why I wrote the third part of this book. *The Payoff*, I called it. Well, it has been for me. I've thoroughly enjoyed writing it for you. Like standing at the top of my personal peak and looking out at a wonderful view, a view that's unique to me, I stand back and see just how far I've come. It's all been worth it. One of the great truths I've realised in writing this is that even though I looked like a thoroughly broken person on pages, pages you've probably found hard to read, I was never broken. The hardships have given me great resources to feel me better and know that I am really engaged with life. My understanding of me and my moments of clarity, of being conscious of who I really am, give me a growing sense of peace. Wasn't it that very witty and insightful man, Oscar Wilde, who said:

"Wherever your life leads you, you must go"

Enjoy that; realise that there is no pressure. Just by being you you've already succeeded. Just play your note, loud and clear, with love and all the great feelings you'd want to have for others and bring to life. What a great way to live!

Then as I stand at this vantage point, this place of quiet and beauty, I get a glimpse of the view ahead. Just a glimpse. It could be the road I travel next, but maybe that's one I can't actually see from where I am now. Right now I feel like doing what many Englishmen do, stop for a cup of tea. Time to enjoy being right here before moving on to see where the path takes me next. "Anything could happen in the next half hour", as an old TV programme from my childhood would say. It would be lovely to live with that sense of adventure, wouldn't it?

Do I live like this all the time? I'd love to say yes. Things are not as rocky as they were. As I understand me better and as I stop resisting or controlling, I find myself in this good place more and more. At this point I could get impatient, like the donkey in the movie *Shrek*. "Are we nearly there yet?" could be constantly on my mind, plaguing me. But there really is nowhere to get to, if, as Steve Jobs, said, "The journey is the reward". So I'm there all the time – except when I'm not!

Of course, the path may seem rugged again at times, but I know that it will lead to more beautiful places, tranquil gardens and more soaring falcons. I look forward to that. In truth, life is just about letting the path open up in front of you as you put one foot in front of the other. That's all exploring is. You, me and everyone are fully qualified to travel with no restrictions. Off we go, on the road trip of a lifetime!

And what of Boiling Frogs? Although the story is commonly known, the amazing thing is that it's not true. It's just a metaphor for life. A delusion. Doesn't that just prove it? It's all a game. Let's all laugh and have fun playing it.

I end this book by asking whether you found your nugget, your one thing that will help you along your way. Maybe it's something you saw in my journey that you've experienced, too. Could it be some little (or big) aha moment when you found yourself agreeing with one of the insights I had on my journey so far? Even if you didn't get your nugget just yet, I'm sure that you will, at some point soon.

On my travels I have come across some eye opening aha moments. I've also had times when my feelings barometer has gone "off the scale" because deep down I've got something on my mind, but I don't know what it is yet. What I learned in those situations was that the realisation will surface, I've just got to relax. It's like swimming in a strong current – no point in fighting it. I have had insights way after the event, too. Again, hindsight is a wonderful thing. How many times have you looked back and laughed at something that seemed serious at the time? You've got it – insights! So even if you don't think you've read anything new here, you probably have.

It's been great to have been a companion with you on your path while you were reading this book. Even if it was only a short time, for me it was worth it. Let me take this opportunity to wish you well as you go on your way. It's uniquely yours. Now I'll grab my shades and put on my helmet, off to ride and enjoy the sunshine – with my girl. Just playing my note. How about you?

Appendix: A New Understanding

(or how to further your understanding of the Principles)

You might be forgiven if you think that me remembering me, remembering who I am, was all the result of things that I did. Taking a road trip, the Bull Run, leaving my family, living in new places and all those circumstances that have been part of this journey. Look a little deeper at what I've written and you'll see the common denominator here is – yes – yours truly. You see, it's all about how we experience life. Everyone does it differently because we are all different, but we all do it the same way, through our thoughts. That's how we interpret the reality that we see, hear, touch, taste, smell and sense around us.

There was a guy called Sydney Banks, a welder from the Northwest Coast of the United States, who had an epiphany one day in the early 1970s, that led to some teachings commonly called the Three Principles of Mind, Consciousness and Thought.

All my discoveries, my journey and the way I live my life now stem from my first discovery of the Three Principles through my great friend and coach Jamie Smart. You can learn the Three Principles very quickly. Book yourself on a weekend workshop, look at some of the great videos online. Try www.livingfromwisdom.com and see Dr Dicken Bettinger sharing his understanding.

There are some great books to read, too. I personally would recommend Michael Neill's book *The Inside-Out Revolution* as one of the best introductions to all of this. My colleague Damian Mark Smyth has written a pretty good book, too, called *Do Nothing*. I guess that's the reason it never occurred to me to write another of those volumes – it's already been done.

For me, there's a much bigger impact that comes from having that initial learning. You get to take that new understanding of how life works and live from that place. That's really what I did during the course of my journey, and it's the way I've been living my life since then. All of the insights that make up Part Three of this book come from noticing life based on my understanding of the principles, and realising how life works for me personally. Some of them will work for you, I hope, but everyone is unique and when you travel this road, the understanding helps you see your life and live in a better way than you ever thought was possible.

Another great experience for me was the Broadband Consciousness course I did with Richard Wilkins and Liz Ivory. It is very similar to the Three Principles in that both teachings are based around the same thing: that your whole experience of life comes from inside of you. You create everything. I highly recommend this course, too. You can book on at www.theministryofinspiration.com or do their online programme at www.thesecretscript.com.

I have created a page called https://www.facebook.com/LifeBeyondMoney , based on this book and dedicated to sharing the lifelong learning from having this understanding. I'd love everyone to benefit, living their life this way. We live our lives that way anyway, whether we've understood the Principles or not, but when you know, you get to see life so much more clearly. It's a wonderful way to live, believe me.

So go take a look at the site or if you just want to start your learning with some research, here are a whole bunch of resources that will set you on your own journey to a new understanding. Enjoy!

In my opinion, the very best resource for understanding the Principles is the original work of Syd Banks, however there are many other sources now available as well as his wonderful books:

Print

The Enlightened Gardener by Syd Banks

The Missing Link by Syd Banks

Second Chance by Syd Banks

Dear Liza by Syd Banks

The Enlightened Gardener Revisited by Syd Banks

In Quest of the Pearl: A Novel by Syd Banks

Somebody Should Have Told Us! by Jack Pransky

The Relationship Handbook by George Pransky

Wisdom for Life: The Principles for Well-Being by Elsie Spittle

Our True Identity...Three Principles by Elsie Spittle

The Inside-Out Revolution by Michael Neill

Supercoach: 10 Secrets to Transform Anyone's Life by Michael Neill

The Spark Inside by Ami Chen Mills-Naim

Parenting from the Heart: A Guide to the Essence of Parenting by Jack Pransky

Modello: A Story of Hope for the Inner City and Beyond by Jack Pransky

Stillpower: The Inner Source of Athletic Excellence by Garret Kramer

The Wisdom Within by Dr Roger Mills & Elsie Spittle

Awareness by Anthony De Mello

Synchronicity: The Inner Path of Leadership by Joseph Jaworski

Do Nothing! by Damian Mark Smyth

Online

A superb resource for Principles training and movies can be found at:

www.threeprinciplesmovies.com

Further required online viewing:

www.inspiringcommunity.org/threeprinciples

www.three-principles.com

www.threeprinciplesresearch.com

www.threeprinciplesfoundation.org

www.3phd.net

www.sydneybanks.org

www.centerforsustainablechange.org

www.sccgov.org

www.starconsultancy.com

www.pranskyandassociates.com

www.insightprinciples.com

www.onethought.com

www.garretkramer.com

www.thethreeprinciples.blogspot.com

www.threeprinciplestraining.com

www.healthrealize.com

www.damianmarksmyth.com

www.facebook.com/pages/Itswhatsinsidethatcounts

Listen (Syd Banks Audios)

All available from www.lonepinepublishing.com

Attitude! (CD-Audio);

Great Spirit (CD-Audio);

Hawaii Lectures (CD-Audio);

In Quest of the Pearl (CD-Audio);

Long Beach Lectures (CD-Audio);

One Thought Away (CD-Audio);

Second Chance (CD-Audio);

Washington Lectures (CD-Audio);

What is Truth? (CD-Audio)

Watch (Syd Banks Videos)

All available from www.lonepinepublishing.com

The Hawaii Lectures (DVD)

#1 - Secret to the Mind

#2 - Oneness of Life

#3 - The Power of Thought

#4 - Going Home

The Long Beach Lectures (DVD)

#1 - The Great Illusion

#2 - Truth Lies Within

#3 - The Experience

#4 - Jumping the Boundaries of Time

The Experience (DVD)

All of these Syd Banks products are available at :

www.sydneybanksproducts.com

Epilogue: 8-3-1

Two years on and another road trip. Same guys as before, plus two, and no destination. This is going to be a real road trip. Just eight of us and our bikes set out for Europe on a one-way Eurostar ticket. That's it. Nothing planned except a vague idea of Rheims the first night.

We get across and quickly get lost not far from Calais. We laugh and joke at our lunch stop. No pressure, but we switch the SatNavs on for the next piece. We've got to get there tonight. I end up leading and I don't realise that the settings on my machine are going to put us on the autoroute. Two hours on the A26, flying in formation through the pouring rain and out the other side. The faithful SatNav finds us a hotel on the outskirts of town, and with a rainbow above us we end our day with our excitement masking the fact that this isn't quite the spontaneity we were hoping for. All that matters is that we are on the road.

A couple of us are keen to ride in the Black Forest. We all know what great roads await, but the forecast is for rain there all week. The weather says head south.

I suggest going to Anthony's in the southwest alps. Bound to be good roads there, we can have a chalet to ourselves and the forecast is good. Sorted ... Except the debate rages about the Black Forest plan. My suggestion is to go with the flow. We get to ride in the Jura and the Alps. But some want to stick with the plan. One of the guys really struggles with dropping the plan. He really wants to risk almost certain wet weather when his mate is recovering from illness and just wants the dry. He wants to stick to roads he knows despite the weather and I sympathise. I've ridden those roads and would gladly go there again – another time! I know this old mistake well now and sit quietly waiting for consensus. Head south. South and sun.

Next day we set out, with the SatNav set for small roads only. Suddenly the ride is exciting. The countryside treats us to bends and straights, towns, rolling countryside and mountains in equal measure. None of us have a clue where we are going, really. We follow our noses and the road trip starts for real.

The Jura don't disappoint and even driving through Geneva in the rush hour in a group of eight is an experience. There are no rules, drive on the kerb, why don't you! Hot work, but fun, too. Gladiators, ARE YOU READY? We are!

The SatNav could never have found the chalet, high on the mountainside like Anthony has arranged. Private dinner, too, prepared by a competition finalist, the food is just great! Everyone is in a party mood now as the drink flows. There's still some talk of heading north again, but I just let that pass. That plan is gone and we all know it really. Who cares about anything but tonight? I get my harmonica out and play along as some of the guys strum guitars that appear, as if by magic, from somewhere in the house. It's a great evening. This was everything I imagined it would be and more. It always amazes me how there is more – when I let it.

Next day starts with another little glitch when Mike's old BMW Thou develops a fault. It's as if we are being guided away from the mountain roads we promised ourselves for today. We need to find a dealer. Ok. I set the SatNav to work and soon we are there. People are hot and energy is low, but we all go with it for Mike's sake.

Hold on, I'm leading the ride again. Was that the plan? I don't mind. I'm just doing what comes to me and everyone seems cool with that for now.

We get to the dealer. It's really hot today. All good as far as I'm concerned, except we should be riding the mountain roads. I don't get stressed like I used to. Plenty of time. The nice technician at the dealer says he won't fix the bike for fear of making a bigger issue. Oh well, it's not terminal. We decide to push on. Mike's going to manage it. Good lad! The guys want to stay by a lake. I get some vague info from the SatNav, and without a clue as to where it leads, we set off. It takes us over a couple of small but wonderful cols to a fantastic lake. The water is so blue at this altitude. I've never seen anything like it. The road trip is unfolding again and we are back on track – or is that off track?

Funny how when you get tired you really feel the heat. The guys are making a hash of finding a hotel for the night, especially as someone has already had a steer from a local. I'm getting cross now. Hot and tired and cross. I just want to stop and get a beer.

Eventually we find our way to a small and very picturesque village I'd spied earlier called Chanaz. The leaders didn't see it. Maybe that's why I'm cross. The hotel there is very basic, but the local restaurant is fantastic. The power of the unknown delivers again: the cols, the lake, the food! Going with the flow delivers again, just as I knew it would.

Simon has to leave the next day and we are seven. It also transpires that the guys who wanted the Black Forest so much have arranged to go back a day early. Without telling anyone. A few of the others want to go with them. Something is telling me to keep heading south. We've got the whole week after all. The Route Napoleon, a famous biker road, beckons and we are game. Suddenly seven become three. Bon Voyage, guys!

The very next day my SatNav gets a glitch and all we can do is operate from an old paper map. Now we really are following our intuition. This is what I call a road trip! Throw the crutch away and walk, Julian!

And I'm not disappointed.   After an interesting lunch in Grenoble – great architecture, local ladies finely dressed and a strange chap on a scooter wants to chat – we head out. The Route Napoleon has the best mix of roads ever! Big wide flowing roads leading us gently and deceptively up and then steeply down with big hairpins. As the altitude drops suddenly the heat returns, one of the joys of riding a bike and being out there in the world.

We don't know it yet, but we are headed for sixty-seven kilometres of the most amazing mountain roads. The road climbs up, hugs the mountainside, high up in the sky, and we seem to go over three summits or more. Now I know how a girl feels experiencing multiple orgasms. Yes, it's that good! I'll remember "the canyon", as the locals call it, for a long, long time.

And then we've done enough. We've not quite made it to the coast, but it's starting to rain and a little hotel in a mountain town seems inviting. It's a lovely place to stop. The three of us are much more comfortable company. There has been no pressure to lead or follow. Just to ride and enjoy.

Next day we play in the hills north of Nice and St Tropez. Canyon roads sinuous at medium speed. Great fun. We know we are headed in roughly the right direction, but we are just loving the bends, the scenery and well, life. We stop for lunch in the square at Salernes and in true French style it takes an hour and a half. I'm not bothered, I'm loving the ride and this new world. It's all so real, here and now. What will we come across next? Exciting.

Suddenly we realise how late we are running. We had half a plan to head for a friend's place in the Pyrenees. For lots of great reasons, but it's a plan, and this is a road trip. Just like our friend earlier, I've fallen into the stick-to-the-plan trap now, and I should know better. We jump on the motorway and start slogging west, getting as far as Nimes before we realise that we just aren't going to make it unless we are very late, and tired, too. But the Carmargue is on the doorstep and we fancy the beach. We ring our apologies through to our friends and promise to visit another time.

As we park the bikes on the dunes at the Grand Traverse we revel in the sea and sunshine. We strip off our leathers for swimming and mojitos on the beach, among the sunbathing beauties. What a way to end the day. Perfect.

Day five starts with us managing to circumnavigate Montpellier to find the road to Millau and the world-famous bridge. We are going to ride it as part of the trip home. The Route Nationale heads on up through the hills. Another sinuous road, but this time a twisting dual carriageway. Another great ride to the top of a plateau where we stop to get fuel and don extra clothing. It's getting cool again. Must be the altitude. We ride on and soon enough we are at the bridge. It's an amazing experience, like being catapulted off a cliff over a huge gorge with the town of Millau down below. Fantastic!

We stop at the visitors' centre briefly and then take the autoroute on up to Clermont-Ferrand. We've got some ground to cover, but it's as we leave the big roads and ride through the Auvergne, destination Chateauroux, that our fun for the day really starts. It's a lovely end to the day. Accommodation proves not to be a problem and we are all set.

The next day the guys set out for Calais and it's just me. Me alone. Flying like a lone eagle through the Loire valley on my way to Nantes. It's wonderful weather and the route is beautiful, too, a mix of fast roads and sightseeing. It feels good to be riding alone. I know exactly what to do. I'm full of confidence, relaxed and thoroughly re-feeling the bike, the roads and freedom. Soaring. This is me.

Saumur is full of people on a sunny Sunday. The Loire is big, beside me most of the way. I skirt the major roads to cross at Pont le Clerc, three bridges with a town on an island in the middle. It's a sunny, beautiful day. Just perfect. I catch an N-road at speed to take me to Nantes. The sun is shining on me in more ways than one now. This is the best ride I've had. I even take a back route to my destination. No problem. I'm completely confident that I can make it despite no directions and only a large-scale map. It's not a problem. Job done.

The next two days I spend with friends, really present in the world. Savouring each moment and loving with a huge sense of contentment and the knowledge that I can't get life wrong. Or maybe it's life that can't get me wrong?

It's time for home. Time to fly once more. I jump on the Blackbird, fill up with gas and off, faster and faster towards the port and my night ferry back home. In my enthusiasm the speed goes up and up. I'm the eagle again, full of power and king of everything I survey. Nearing Caen I notice that fuel is running short. I take a small detour but don't find a station, and then, two kilometres from the port I run out of fuel.

I'm on my own in a foreign country with no idea exactly where I am, which makes it tricky to get help. The bike just needs fuel. There was a time when this would have been a drama for me, but I just go with the flow. Eventually, after talking to a French policeman who doesn't speak any English, pushing my fully loaded bike a kilometre and persuading a local driver to let me use his bankcard in return for cash, I have fuel. There's still time.

I ride to the port. The ferry is still docked and I remonstrate with the guys at the barrier, but they don't let me through. "Boarding is closed", they say firmly in their best English. They point me to the terminal and the guy there books me on tomorrow's boat at no extra charge and into a local hotel. As I leave the ferry area to mount up I look to the skies and laugh. I'm happy with life and this is just a little inconvenience. All part of the trip. Fun. The hidden bonus is my cabin next morning. Big spacious and with a bed and a shower after a late night and an early start, I go to bed at eight in the morning and the boat rocks me to sleep.

Wonderful. Who could ask for more? But more there is.

I ride the English country back roads with ease, straight to the pub for lunch and my family are there to greet me with hugs and smiles. Once again I know that life is here for me. Right here, right now. I know who I am much more deeply than before, although I always knew really. I'm ready for life. There's nothing to do, no place to go, wonderful ...

"*Jonathan sighed and looked out to sea. 'You don't need me any longer. You need to keep finding yourself, a little more each day. That real, unlimited Fletcher Seagull. He's your instructor. You need to understand him and practice him.'*"

Richard Bach, *Jonathan Livingstone Seagull*

If you have enjoyed

Life Beyond Money

And you want to live from a new understanding visit:

www.livingfromwisdom.com

to join my mailing list and receive information

about further publications and courses visit:

https://www.facebook.com/LifeBeyondMoney

I welcome your feedback. Please post your review on Amazon.

See your stories for what they really are and start living

..I mean really living!

Julian